today
is
the
only
day!

today is the only day!

Herb Sadler

Ardara House, Publishers
1500 East Johnson Avenue, Suite 123
Pensacola, FL 32514
850 479 7962

Today is the Only Day!

© 1997 by W. Herbert Sadler, Jr. All rights reserved.

No part of this work may be reproduced or transmitted in any form or by any means, electronic or mechanical, including photocopying and recording, or by any information storage or retrieval system except as may be expressly permitted by the 1976 Copyright Act or in writing from the author. Requests for permission should be addressed in writing to Herb Sadler, 75 Fairpoint Road, Gulf Breeze, Florida 32561.

In not using capital letters for pronouns that refer to the deity, the editors have followed the style utilized in the King James Version and the New Revised Standard Version of the scriptures. We have set in italics direct quotations from the Old Testament and the New Testament.

Library of Congress Catalog Card Number: 97-73789
ISBN: 1888676035

To

My Parents
Billy and Elizabeth Sadler

for their love, encouragement,
and example

Table of Contents

11	Today is the Only Day!
21	Choosing Life's Foundations
27	Planning for Tomorrow
35	Overcoming Failure
45	Overcoming Fatigue
55	Overcoming Adversity
65	Overcoming Stress
77	Overcoming Temptation
87	Practicing Perseverance
95	Practicing Patience
105	Using What God Has Given
113	Dealing With Difficult People
125	Receiving and Sharing Love
133	Getting Through to Loved Ones
141	Seeing and Seizing the Future

Preface

Some people are prone to live life looking backward. They yearn for the good old days, or they continue to bemoan mistakes and failures. Either way, their focus is on life already lived.

My tendency is to place too much emphasis on the future, to spend an inordinate amount of time planning, preparing, anticipating. In the language of Robert Hastings' classic parable, "The Station," I'm prone to fix my attention on the destination (the Station), and I miss the joy of the journey.

My hope is that this book will help you remember, as it does me, the simple, practical, and profound truth: today is the only day we have to find joy and meaning. *This is the day the Lord has made; let us rejoice and be glad in it* (Psalm 118:24).

I am deeply grateful to the members of the most extraordinary local church I know, the Gulf Breeze United Methodist Church, in Gulf Breeze, Florida, for their support and encouragement through twenty-three years of loving and serving Jesus Christ together.

A special thanks to Amy Baker, my remarkable secretary, for her help in the preparation of this manuscript and for all she does to extend my ministry and the ministry of our church. An equal thanks goes to George Baskin, my publisher, who pushes me to put into print the message of God's grace and who then helps me do it.

Finally, thanks to all of you who had such kind words about *We Can All Be Winners!*. Your generous words of support made it so much easier to prepare this further word from the Lord: *Today is the Only Day!*

Today is the Only Day!

Psalms 118:24

Gene Stallings was until recently the head football coach at the University of Alabama. In 1993 he coached the Alabama team that won the national championship. Stallings is not only a great football coach but a man who represents many of humanity's highest values. In his incredibly moving book *Another Season*—published this year—Stallings tells about the birth of his son. One of the doctors came out and said to him, not only abruptly but I would say cruelly, "You have a son, but he is a mongoloid." The doctors told the stunned coach that John Mark had Down Syndrome—a genetic condition that causes mental retardation—and would perhaps live as long as four years.

After he passed the age of four, doctors revised the number to eleven. John Mark is now thirty-four years old. His physical condition is not good. He has some heart problems. His days, in fact, are now probably very limited. But he has lived and worked in ways that people thought impossible.

Stallings tells the remarkable outcome of love a day at a time: "John Mark is not worried about a national championship; he wants the team to win because it makes Pop happy. That's what I love about him. I learned about unconditional love from Johnny. I try not to think about how much time he has remaining. I just appreciate every day we have together."

As point guard on the basketball team at Duke University, Bobby Hurley, an unassuming young man from New Jersey, provided the leadership and the inspiration for three Final Four appearances and consecutive national championships. His high school team had gone 32-0 and was ranked No. 1 in the nation. In 1993 he was a first-round draft selection of the Sacramento *Kings* and, even though a rookie, became a starter. Shortly afterwards, Bobby Hurley was almost killed as he drove home in his pickup truck after a game. An automobile without lights crashed into him as he made a legal left turn at an intersection. He was thrown from the truck into a ditch and lay, face down, in several inches of water. He probably would have drowned if he had not been rescued by an off-duty policeman. Bobby's injuries were so severe that it was not at all certain he would live. He was in the intensive care unit with broken ribs, a detached trachea, collapsed lungs, possibly a broken neck.

His family back in New Jersey asked for prayers. People all over the country began praying for him. As a result of prayers, excellent care, and his fitness before the injury, Bobby Hurley began to heal miraculously. When he left the hospital—wearing sunglasses and a Santa hat!—he said: "The wreck has changed my whole perspective on life. I had been depressed about how the Sacramento *Kings* were doing and about problems with my family, but now every day I'm just happy to wake up. My priorities have changed dramatically."

Bobby Hurley got a wake-up call which said to him, "This is the day the Lord has made. Rejoice and be glad in it!" Before the accident, he was like the rest of us: every day a day to try to attack some difficulty, every day a day to cope with hardship. It's as if a cloud descends upon us and we can no longer see the horizon. While the cloud of problems from yesterday engulfs us, we hope that there may be better times over the horizon tomorrow.

Yet we can't count on happiness to begin some time off in the future. It is intended by God to begin for you and for me this very day. We do not have to experience tragedy to hear God's wake-up call for every one of us.

> **Today is the only day we have**

We don't have yesterday; it's gone.
We don't have tomorrow; it may or may not come.
All we really have is today.

God himself exists in the present. In the Book of Exodus (3:13-14) God is asked "What is your name?" He answers, "My name is 'I am.'" God doesn't say his name is "I was." He doesn't say his name is "I will be." God says "I am, I am." You and I exist in the present, as well, so if we are to have the happiness and joy that God intends for us to have, we have to have them today.

When I was twelve or thirteen my family got our first television set, a black and white set with a round screen. That was one of the monumental days of my childhood and youth! It was a big occasion for us all. My favorite show, "The Mickey Mouse Club," came on in the afternoon after school was over, so I was home in time to see it. It was my favorite, not because of the cartoons or the adventure stories but because of Annette. I couldn't wait to see those mouseketeers line up and peel off, one by one, as they gave their names—just to see that incredible smile and hear her call out "Annette!" That was a long, long time ago, but to this day when there's anything in the news about Annette Funicello, I look and I listen and I read.

I was fascinated in July, 1992, when she revealed in a press conference that she has multiple sclerosis. She said this: "I've had it for five years. I didn't go public for a long time because I believed people want to think nothing bad ever happens to Annette."

Well, bad things do happen, to Annette and to Gene Stallings and to Bobby Hurley and to you and to me. If they haven't yet, they will. We must learn to live each day triumphantly. Today is the only day we have.

> **Claim today as
> the day of the Lord's victory**

Today is the Only Day!

We have a tendency to see our problems so clearly we forget that if we'll simply look at life differently, it will be different. Then we can see the other side of it, the side that's good. Maybe you heard about the guy whose wife met him at the door and said, "Dear, I have good news or I have bad news. Which would your prefer?"

He replied, "It's been a real rough day. I want the good news."

She said, "The good news is the air bags on our new car work."

It's all in how you look at it. You can focus on the down side, or you can recognize the up side. You can claim the good news that God does something good in every single circumstance. No matter what your situation, there is a way that you can look at your life and see God's victory and claim goodness and joy and peace and meaning right now. No matter how young you are or how old. No matter what kind of condition you find yourself in. I can illustrate that point by telling about POWs or people in concentration camps, people in the worst kind of confinement, who with the grace and power and peace of God in their hearts and in their lives, have found meaning even within that imprisonment, even in that limited and confined circumstance.

While most of us will never experience that kind of imprisonment, life sometimes places us in a different kind of confinement. Elsie McClay has written *Green Winters*, a book about a woman confined in a nursing home. Her moving words are something of a prayer.

Preserve me from the occupational therapist, God. She means well, but I'm too busy to make baskets. I want to relive a day in July when Sam and I went berrying.

I was eighteen. My hair was long and thick and I braided it and wound it around my head so it wouldn't get caught in the briars. But when we sat down in the shade to rest I unpinned it and it came tumbling down, and Sam proposed. I suppose it wasn't fair to use my hair to make him fall in love with me, but it was a good marriage.

Oh, here comes the therapist with scissors and paste. "Would I like to decoupage?"

"No," I say, "I haven't got time."

"Nonsense," she says, "you're going to live a long, long time."

That's not what I mean. I mean that all my life I've been doing things for people, with people. I have to catch up on my thinking, feeling—about Sam's death, for one thing. At the time there were so many things to do, so many people around, I had to keep assuring everyone I'd be alright. I had to eat. And make sure they noticed that I ate so they wouldn't keep coming to see me when they had other things to do. I had to comfort the children and I had to comfort Sam's old friends because they got scared. After all, if Sam could die, they could die too. And I had to give his clothes away and pay the bills and I didn't have much time to think about how brave he was and how sweet.

One day, close to end, I asked if there was anything I could do for him.

"Yes," he said. "Unpin your hair."

I said, "Oh, Sam, it's so thin now, and gray."

"Please," he said, "unpin it anyway."

I did and he reached out his hand, skin transparent. I could see the blue veins, and he stroked my hair. If I close my eyes, I can feel it. Sam.

"Please open your eyes," the therapist says. "You don't want to sleep the day away."

As I say, she means well. She wants to know what I used to do—knit, crochet? Yes, I did those things, and cooked and cleaned and raised five children, and had things happen to me, beautiful things and terrible things. I need to think about them. At the time, there wasn't time. I need to sort them out, arrange them on the shelves of my mind.

I love that story because it demonstrates so beautifully that no matter what our circumstances are, no matter what our limits are—physically or otherwise—we can make this the day of the Lord's victory. We can make this a day to celebrate and find meaning.

I admired and appreciated C.S. Hodge, who died recently at ninety-three years of age. At the end of every year he sent a newsletter out to his friends all across the country. One of the things he talked about in his last newsletter was how wonderful the new church organ is. In a paragraph about the old organ is a sentence that arrested my attention. Our minister of music had done CPR on that organ time and time again and brought it back to life and gotten it going. C.S. wrote, "The old organ died right in the middle of the Doxology." I hadn't thought about that, but that's exactly how it happened. We were singing, "Praise God from whom all blessings flow." And the organ coughed once and died. I thought, when I read C.S.'s words, that's how I want to go. I want to go singing, "Praise God from whom all blessings flow." I want to go living the Doxology. The only way to do that is to start living it now!

This is the day the Lord has made! Rejoice and be glad in it!

Choosing Life's Foundations
Matthew 7:24-27

The young man didn't know what he wanted to do with his life. He had graduated from Cal-State Fullerton with a degree in business, but he knew that he didn't want a coat-and-tie, nine-to-five job. He took such a job, however, and lasted just a month with it. After he floundered around for a while, he finally fell on his knees and prayed for direction: "Oh Lord, show me what I ought to do."

Eventually Kevin Cosner came to understand what he was to do with his life. He had become an actor and ultimately a director, but his mission became to elevate the standards of the movie industry. He resolved to make a difference artistically but add a moral component. He did just that with a beautiful film, a fable entitled *Field of Dreams*, a story of baseball and relationships and eternity.

Then Cosner had a vision of a film he wanted to make about the soul of the Native American. It would be called *Dances With Wolves*. Financing for the project was difficult to get because there hadn't been a successful western in twenty-five years. He knew that his prospective sponsors would not like that this movie was going to be three hours long, at least an hour longer than the movies which were commercial successes. Also, much of it was going to have subtitles in a Native American dialect.

There were many obstacles, but he finally found the money to begin the project. One critical scene was to involve hundreds of running buffalo, but those who had put up the money said it was unnecessary and too expensive. Cosner scraped up the required millions of dollars from his own personal assets and he filmed his movie, his way.

With his personal mission always before him, this man took the risk and did something he truly believed in. In the end, he was not disappointed. The movie of his vision was nominated for twelve academy awards and won seven, including best picture of the year and director of the year for Cosner himself.

Choosing Life's Foundations

Jesus tells the story of two home builders (Matthew 7:24-27). One built his house on a very solid foundation. One built his house upon a shaky foundation. There was an enormous difference in what happened after the homes were completed. One outcome was happy, the other tragic. The difference was not determined by whether or not the storms came, for the storms came to both the wise and the foolish builder. The difference was in the vision for the future.

Jesus makes it clear that the successful builder was a person who could envision what might happen and would prepare. The wise builder, he said, foresaw the possibility of the storm and planned for it. To use a phrase made famous by Stephen Covey, he began with the end in mind.

Dr. Charles Garfield made an extensive study of peak performers when he worked with astronauts in the NASA Space Program to determine what enables certain people to excel. Then he studied people who have excelled in various other fields—business, science and sports. He found that almost all of them were visualizers. They were people who could see it before it happened. They were people who began with the end in mind.

It can be the same thing with your life. Decide where God wants you to be—in your spiritual life, your

Today is the Only Day!

economic life, your home life, your relational life, your *whole* life. Begin with the end in mind. Then put into place those things that get you from here to there. I know little about computers, but I know some things about human beings, and this I know. You are the programmer of your own life. God can supply the components, but you implement the program. The key to success is being true to that vision which will control your life.

Ernest Campbell told a story about a lonely woman who went to a pet shop and bought a parrot to keep her company. After a couple of days she came back and complained to the sales lady, "This parrot won't talk."

The salesperson said, "Does it have a mirror? You know parrots like to be able to see themselves and they talk if they can see themselves."

So the woman bought a mirror. But the next day she came back. "The parrot still won't talk."

"Does it have a ladder?" asked the saleslady. "You know parrots like little ladders so they can hop up and down."

She bought a ladder, but the next day she came back. "The parrot still won't talk."

"A swing," the sales person said. "A swing so the parrot can sit up there and just swing back and forth."

She bought a swing. But the next day the woman was back to announce that the bird had died.

"Oh, I'm so sorry," said the saleslady. "Did it ever say anything?"

"As a matter of fact, it did. Just before it died, it said, 'Don't they sell any food down there?'"

We surround ourselves with things that please us and amuse us while we neglect the priority items which form the foundation of productive living. When you envision the mission of your own life, ask yourself the question, "What will my life be like if I continue to build it on shaky foundations? How will I get rid of the sand on which my life is built?"

As you prioritize your life, begin with the Creator of your life. As you decide what is really important and what you are going to give your future to, rely on the One who forgives your sins and restores you after you make a mistake. As you prioritize your life, place God Almighty and his Kingdom first because he is the foundation that supports the structure of the rest of life. Today is the only day you and I have to build the strong house that will shelter us during the storms of the future.

Planning for Tomorrow

Philippians 3:12-14; Matthew 6:34

The Psalmist said, *Where there is no vision, people perish.* The great preacher Halford Luccock told a story about a New England village. The townspeople were informed that a power dam would be built on a river nearby, creating a lake which would inundate their homes. Money would be provided for them to relocate within about one year. Luccock observed that some of the houses needed a coat of paint, but nobody painted. Some screen doors were torn, but no one made repairs. A number of homeowners didn't even cut their lawns that year. Things were generally left in a state of disrepair. Describing the situation, Luccock made a statement which I thought was profound. He said, "Where there is no hope for the future, there is no power in the present."

I very often spend time with cancer patients and others with life-threatening illnesses. I recognize how very necessary it is for them to continue to believe in the future, to continue to have a sense of tomorrow because when there is no belief in tomorrow there is no hope for the present.

Almost a half-century ago, seven people in Gulf Breeze, Florida, decided to plan for building a Methodist church in their town. Seven people. Visionary people who decided to look to tomorrow. They made possible a place which is now the place for worship and fellowship and love and sharing for over three thousand people.

It's important to believe in tomorrow and to plan for it. That's one of the reasons churches have Christian Education. They plan for Sunday School classes and other small group opportunities so that persons can learn the faith which will help them live out the days to come.

For years my favorite comic strip was "Calvin and Hobbs." Calvin is a rather precocious lad, very imaginative. Hobbs is a toy stuffed tiger when Calvin's parents are around, but when nobody else is there, Hobbs is a real tiger. He and Calvin play together and communicate with each other. Hobbs is rather like Calvin's alter-ego. Where Calvin is selfish, Hobbs is generous. Calvin is impulsive, but Hobbs is careful and wise. One day as Calvin and Hobbs are walking along together,

Calvin says, "Live for the moment is my motto. You never know how long you've got. Why, you could be walking along, step out into the road and wham! get hit by a cement truck. Then you'd be sorry you put off all your pleasures. Yep, that's what I say. Live for the moment. That's my motto. What's your motto?"

Hobbs says, "Look down the road."

The wisdom of Hobbs' reply lies at two levels. On the first level, he's saying if you look down the road and see what the circumstances may be for any particular behavior, then you might wisely choose not to engage in that behavior. You can spare yourself much hardship if you'll look down the road and see what happens to people who engage in those kinds of activities. But there is a second and deeper wisdom in Hobbs' motto. It means also to look into the future, see the outcome that God is going to bring to pass, and claim that victory for yourself now.

Planning for tomorrow and beyond is vital, but there's another side of this same truth that gives us balance: we live today. Jesus said don't worry about tomorrow. *Take no thought for tomorrow*, the King James Version of the Bible reads. The New Revised Standard Version translates it this way: "*So do not worry* about tomorrow, for tomorrow will bring worries of its own. Today's trouble is enough for today" (Matthew 6:34).

Bishop Ernest Fitzgerald tells of a man who, some years ago, visited the western North Carolina mountains and decided that those mountainsides would be a wonderful place to grow grapes and make wine. He gathered a group of the local people together, but he couldn't get them to visualize the great benefits of the future he was talking about. They just weren't interested, even though he used his finest sales pitch: "Join me and in three or four years you'll be so well fixed you'll never have to worry again."

There was long silence and then one mountaineer drawled, "I ain't worryin' none now."

I suspect all of us have known people like that, people so tranquil and poised that they were not disturbed or concerned about what might happen in the future. At my grandmother's knee I heard her whisper in my ear many times, "This is the day the Lord has made; let us rejoice and be glad in it." Today is to be celebrated, for it is what we have.

My favorite young movie critic, our son, Scott, recommended a movie entitled *Dead Poets Society*. He said it was a great movie with a great message. He was right. It's a story about an English teacher who goes to teach at an exclusive prep school. When he receives his class of young boys on their first day, he invites them out into the hallway, where there are photographs of students from years gone by, all the way back beyond the turn of the century. He says to these young students, "Step forward and see these faces from the past." So they examine closely the faces of then-young men, bright with hope. "They were just like you are now. They believed they were destined for great things. Look at their eyes. But, gentlemen, these boys whose pictures you look at are now fertilizing daffodils. If you listen closely, you will hear them whisper their legacy to you. Let's listen to what they are whispering."

And they all leaned forward to hear. In a sepulchral voice the teacher says, "'Seize the day!' This is their message to you. 'Seize the day!'"

It's how you live today that will determine the quality of tomorrow. Do you understand that? It's how you live today that will determine the quality of tomorrow.

Dennis Waitley brought that point home to me when I read the account of his interview with some prisoners of war from Vietnam. Air Force Lieutenant Colonel George Hall said that he spent five and one-half years as a prisoner of war, most of that time in solitary confinement.

What does one do in solitary confinement for five and one-half years? Well, mostly one thinks. George Hall said, "I could have filled my mind with my fears, my concerns, my worries, my anxieties about the future, or I could fill my mind with those things which were positive and tranquil and rewarding for me. I chose to do the latter. Every day for five and one-half years I played a round of golf in my mind."

One day he would play Pebble Beach, and the next he would play Augusta National, or the old course at St. Andrews. He would step up to the first blue tee—the back tee, the championship tee—and take out of his golf bag a brand new Titlest golf ball. He would tee the ball, take a couple of practice swings with his driver and drive the ball long and true down the center of the fairway. It would hit on that plush green grass, bounce a few times, roll, and come to a stop.

And then George Hall would walk from the tee to his ball. He would take out an iron or a wood, whatever was appropriate, and he would strike the ball again. He always replaced his divot, he always replaced his ball mark on the green, and he always raked the traps. When he was on the green, he would line up his putt, crouching down, checking the break, checking the speed, checking the distance, and he would putt. When he would finish with that hole, he would replace the pole. Then he would go to the next tee, put his golf ball in the ball washer and clean his ball before playing the second and subsequent holes.

Every day, there in the prison camp, he played golf in his mind. Every day for five and one-half years. After George Hall was released by the Vietnamese, within a week of having arrived back in this country, he was invited to play in the Pro-Am for the New Orleans Open and was paired with the professional Orville Moody. Lt. Colonel Hall had not been on an actual golf course in seven years, but he teed it up and shot 76. Exactly on his four handicap. The photographers thought his game was amazing. "Beginner's re-entry luck," they said.

George Hall said, "No. For the last five years I have not three-putted a green once."

It's how you live today that will determine the quality of tomorrow. Whether you are living today in a concentration camp, whether you are living today in a despicable situation relationally, whether your job is not to your liking—whatever your circumstance—it's how you think, it's how you feel, it's the quality of your faith, it's your relationship with God that determines the quality of your life.

Happiness does not depend upon the condition of marriage. Happiness does not depend upon the condition of financial stability. Happiness does not depend upon the condition of job security! It does not depend upon parenting. It does not depend upon any condition. Happiness is a quality of the soul, of the spirit. And if you have that, then you are happy in any condition.

Our Lord Jesus Christ gives to us that condition of the heart which makes possible happiness in every circumstance. So let us, as the Bible advises, plan for tomorrow and beyond tomorrow, but let us understand that God gives us today in which to live.

Overcoming Failure

Matthew 10:5-14

A few years ago, planning a talk on failure, I decided I would base the introduction on the results of an Orange Bowl game which would be played the day before I would give the talk. A Florida football team—either Florida State University or the University of Miami—was going to win a national NCAA championship and the other was going to lose it. What better introduction for a talk on failure?

The only problem was that I had to change that introduction four times in the last minute and a half of the game! Fans on each side took turns celebrating what they thought would be a certain win. FSU's coach Bobby Bowden (a staunch Baptist, by the way, and a thoroughly Christian gentleman) even received a premature Methodist baptism of Gatorade!

In the final moments the outcome would depend on a field goal attempt from the FSU forty-five yard line. Watching the game on television, I became tense all over as I comprehended the awesome responsibility resting on the shoulders (or in the leg) of a young Miami place kicker from the Midwest. Bryon Bennett could win a national championship for his team and his school and all the alumni and fans, as well as a great deal of fame and notoriety for himself. Or he could lose it.

The FSU fans went wild as the ball sailed wide left of the goal posts. I had my introduction, all right, and a powerful lesson on failure. Sometimes we win and sometimes we lose. Sometimes we succeed and sometimes we fail.

There are all kinds of failures. There are relational failures and business failures, but the most significant, long-term, are moral and spiritual failures. And they come about as a result of the lack of moral and spiritual discipline in our lives.

A little boy who was in an airplane for the very first time, enjoyed looking out at the landscape below. As the plane passed over a wide and meandering river, he asked, "Daddy, what makes the river so crooked?"

His father's answer was right on target: "The river is crooked because it follows the path of least resistance."

Crooked lives are made the same way. It's no accident that the words *discipline* and *disciple* are so similar. If you and I are to be disciples of Jesus Christ, we may do so only if we lead morally and spiritually disciplined lives. We must base our decisions from this time forward on principles, on standards, on our faith, and not on feelings. Moral decisions that are based on feelings very often turn into experiences of shame, regret and remorse. Feelings are fickle. Feelings change. But standards—what we believe in, what Jesus Christ teaches us to do—are immovable and we may never have to live with shame if we uphold them.

ADMIT YOUR FAILURE

There's no way to deal with failure or move beyond it until first we acknowledge that it is *our* failure. Not everybody is willing to do that. Too many times we blame someone else: it's his fault or it's her fault or it's their fault or it's the boss's fault or it's the employee's fault or it's the government's fault.

Another common way of dealing with failure is fatalism: it's God's fault; it's in the stars. Some people deal with failure by practicing self-pity: I'm a victim—poor, pitiful me; my experiences from my childhood made me this way. None of those attempts to deal with failure are healthy or helpful. To move beyond failures we have to admit them and take responsibility.

I think it was Jim Moore who told about answering his phone one night and hearing this sweet, elderly voice. "May I please speak to Martha?"

Jim said, "I'm sorry, ma'am, but there's no one here by that name."

A sudden click and the line went dead. In just a little while the phone rang again, and the same voice on the other end of the line said, "May I please speak to Martha?"

And Jim said again, with patience, "I'm sorry, ma'am, but there is no one at this residence by that name."

Click.

The third time the telephone rang, the same voice asked, "May I please speak to Martha?"

With a little less patience this time, Jim said, "Ma'am, there is no one here named Martha. I think you are dialing the wrong number."

She said, "I am not dialing the wrong number. You're answering the wrong phone."

Sometimes we just don't want to admit it when it's our fault.

George McDonald was a British preacher and writer of the late nineteenth century. One day his elders, the church leaders, came to him and said, "George, we have to inform you that we can no longer pay your salary."

That night, when he was telling his wife about the experience, he said, "I've thought about it and I've prayed about it and I've decided that I can really make a living with my writing and my teaching. I've decided that I'm going to stay on as the pastor here without salary and continue to serve these people."

She was wiser and had more sensitivity and awareness than he did. Putting her hand on his hand, she said, "George, it's not that these people are too poor to pay us. It's that they don't want us."

As painful as it is, the beginning place for dealing with failure is to face it, to acknowledge it, to admit it.

MOVE ON PAST YOUR FAILURE

In the tenth chapter of the gospel of Matthew, Jesus gives important advice to those seventy-two he sent out:

when you fail, when what you are trying to do is rejected, shake the dust from your feet and go to the next place. He said, As you enter the house, greet it. If the house is worthy, let your peace come upon it; but if it is not worthy, let your peace return to you.

Referring to this passage, my mentor, Carlyle Marney, used the expression "the sacrament of failure." It's rather like a sacrament, a symbolic act which realizes in us a great spiritual reality.

When you fail, move on past it. Actually experience that symbolic act of shaking the dust from your feet. Shake that failure from your own being, from your experience, and move to the next place.

Every person fails. But we have to move beyond the failure and not get stuck there. A great business leader has this message in needlepoint on the wall of his office: *Babe Ruth struck out 1,330 times.* All of us strike out occasionally, when what we need is a home run. Babe Ruth reminds us that we can get beyond yet another strike-out.

A famous Texas oil man said, "When I drill a dry hole, I fill it with concrete and walk away." Some of us are looking at dry holes when we expected gushers. The oil man's example tells us that staring at a dry hole is useless. It's much better to shake that dust from our feet and move on.

LEARN FROM YOUR FAILURE

Once we acknowledge failure, we may be able to learn from it. A failure analyzed and understood could be an experience from which we can profit greatly. Some years ago chemists for the 3M company were experimenting with a bonding agent. They wanted a super-adhesive product for an industrial bonding purpose, but what they came up with didn't work. It would stick, but it wouldn't stick well. And so they put this idea on the shelf. Later, one of those chemists, a church choir singer, was having difficulty with the little pieces of paper he used to mark pages in his hymnal and his choir folder. They kept slipping out. He remembered the stuff his laboratory made that would stick but not well, and Post-it Notes is now a multi-million-dollar business. It didn't stick very well; it was a failure. It doesn't stick very well; it is a great success.

The great men and women of history have not been people who never failed. Rather, they have been people who failed and learned from those experiences.

Today is the Only Day!

Thomas Edison had very little schooling. He was a newsboy on the Grand Trunk Railroad and later a telegraph operator in various cities. He was a failure at selling newspapers to persons traveling on the train and was not much better at being a telegraph operator. But his first inventions were the transmitter and receiver for the automatic telegraph and an improved stock-ticker system. Edison's phonograph was the first successful instrument of its kind. He produced the first commercially practical incandescent lamp in 1879. And that was just the beginning. Talking pictures were based on his work. And the telephone. He held more than thirteen hundred U.S. and foreign patents. But in all this time, during intensive work in the laboratory, he actually had more failures than he did successes.

John Wesley, the founder of Methodism, traveled from England to Georgia as a missionary to convert the Indians. He returned without starting a church, without converting one Indian, without establishing one Christian person in this country. He went home a failure. But he learned from those failure experiences, and his legacy is The Methodist Church with millions and millions of members world-wide.

Victor Hugo had been hailed in France as the greatest poet of his day. But when he was forty-eight, his political support of Napoleon III got him into trouble and he was banished to the island of Guernsey. It was there in exile that he wrote his classic novel, *Les Miserables*.

Much of our failure we can learn from and profit from if we are willing to do so. The hardest part may be admitting and owning up to it. But once that part is done, we can move past it and—having learned from the experience—make something good happen.

The earthly ministry of Jesus Christ might have seemed to be the greatest failure of all times. He came preaching and teaching and healing, and when he had done all this and was put to death on a hill outside Jerusalem, there were only a few women and one man present to mourn his passing. So far as we know, not a single other supporter of Jesus came out to be with him at the hour of his death. But God took that failure and turned it into the experience of God's greatest victory and—more—the greatest victory for our lives. It is the means whereby the slate of yesterday's failures is wiped clean for us. Christ's "failure" is the means by which we can overcome our own failures this very day.

Overcoming Fatigue
I Kings 19

I heard a story about a truck driver who puzzled the other drivers on the road. He would drive about five miles down the highway, then stop, leap out of the cab to pound on the side of the truck, jump back in, and drive a little farther. He would pull off again after another few miles and repeat the same process, pounding on the side of the truck, then jumping back in the cab to drive on. The man driving the automobile behind him watched for a while, and the next time the truck driver stopped he pulled off also.

"Why do you keep stopping and hitting your truck?"

The perspiring truck driver explained, "I'm carrying a ton of canaries in this half-ton truck and I have to keep half of them in the air all the time."

I've had exactly that feeling at times, like I'm juggling more things than I can hold in my hands and I have to keep them in the air all the time or they will crash down on me. Harriet Beecher Stowe in *Uncle Tom's Cabin* wrote, "I'm tired way down into the future." Have you ever felt like that? An absolute over-fatigue. A fatigue you can't identify the source of.

Peter DeVries, the novelist, said, "Novels, life-like novels, have three parts—a beginning, a muddle, and an ending." Some of us find ourselves in the muddle of life and what do we do?

The story of Elijah the Prophet in the nineteenth chapter of I Kings helps us to answer that question. Elijah had just completed the greatest victory of his life. He had defeated the prophets of Baal on Mount Carmel, all by himself, one against four hundred. Then he had them taken down to the Wadi Kishon and there killed all four hundred of them. As a result, Queen Jezebel told him that she would have him killed.

So Elijah fled for his life. He was so terrified he walked over a hundred miles to Beersheba, then another day's journey out into the country. Exhausted, both because of his efforts at Mount Carmel and because of the trip, he sat down under the shade of a solitary broom tree. Despondent, he said to God, "It's too much, Lord. I might as well be dead."

What's happening here? What's going on with Elijah? First of all, he's physically tired. He's just worn out. He had the exhausting time with the prophets of Baal, and then he killed all four hundred of them with the sword, and then he walked over a hundred miles in the heat of Palestine. Second, he's mentally exhausted. Anyone who thinks he might as well be dead is depressed. Third, Elijah is spiritually bankrupt, even though only a short time before he had achieved his greatest victory on God's behalf.

This story has a lot to say to you and me about times when we get fatigued. First of all, when we are overcome with physical fatigue, we need the rest. We all need regular periods of rest and relaxation.

I heard about the church member who was mad at his pastor. This member called the church office on Monday and was told that the preacher was not there. So he called back on Tuesday and said accusingly, "I tried to reach you yesterday and you were not there."

"Well, Monday is my day off."

"The devil doesn't take a day off."

I like the minister's answer. He said, "That's right. And if I didn't, I'd be just like him."

The word "Sabbath" identifies that period of time when God himself rested after his labor. God's example says to you and me that there needs to be a rhythm to life, a time to work and a time to rest. Sometimes when our strength seems to run out but the task hasn't, we say, "I don't have time to stop and rest." That's simply not true. Someone said if we don't have a time to come apart, then we come apart. You owe it to yourself and to your work to have periods when you just lay down your tasks and rest.

Sometimes fatigue is emotional. There is more and more evidence that our emotional condition is a strong influence on our physical condition. When Elijah says to God, "Take my life," we know that much of his problem is emotional.

What can you and I do when the weariness we feel is a mental weariness? First, we can claim the power of a positive attitude. The American Psychological Association published a report which says that by the year 2000 medical work-up forms will contain a strong section having to do with attitudes. The report states that hostile, suspicious people have poorer health than people who are more trusting. It says that pessimists encounter more health problems than optimistic persons who start out no healthier. When confronted with stress, those who interpret change as a challenge fare much better healthwise than people who are fearful of change. We can bring a new physical power into our lives by emotionally claiming the power of a positive attitude.

We can also claim the power that comes from knowing that there is purpose in our lives. A direction, a goal, a destination will lift many burdens. A stonecutter was given detailed instructions and sketches for some carvings, which he followed, even though he could not understand how his work would fit into whatever was being built. Later, as he saw his own work used in a lovely cathedral, he commented, "My hand would have been steadier and my work easier if I had known why I was working."

When we know what our direction is and the purpose of our lives, much of the weariness is lifted from our shoulders and we find a new strength to go on.

One of the great spiritual giants of this century was E. Stanley Jones. I had the privilege, when I was a college student, of hearing Stanley Jones preach at Huntingdon College in Montgomery, Alabama. I remember that before I heard him speak, I was struck by one fact that impressed me more than all his religious credentials: at the age of seventy-two this man still did one hundred push-ups a day!

When E. Stanley Jones was a young man, he went to India as a missionary to convert the intellectuals of that nation, but he suffered a nervous breakdown. After a period of rejuvenation he returned to his work but became ill again. This time he came home to the United States to recover but eventually went back and subsequently had two more emotional breakdowns. Finally, one night in the city of Lucknow, Stanley Jones buried his head in his hands and said, "Lord I can't do it! I can't go on any longer." It was then, he said, that "I heard a voice—not an audible one—but it was clear to me that God was speaking: 'Stanley, do you want to do the work I've given you to do? If you will turn yourself over to me, I will give you all the energy you need for all the days you live upon the earth.'"

Stanley Jones said that, as a result of his experience that night in the city of Lucknow, he was never tired again for forty years. Isn't that remarkable?

Dr. Jones' story says to me that the Christian faith is more than principles or the teachings of Jesus on a printed page. The Christian faith is about a power that lifts persons up and that will meet our every need. It is available to us always for energy, both physical and emotional.

Sometimes when we are tired we think we are alone. Part of Elijah's problem was that he believed he was all alone. But he wasn't. God tells him, "Elijah, I've got seven thousand other people who are with you, and you just don't know it. They are there, they are supporting you, they are about the same work that you are."

I find that very often people feel alone when they aren't. They feel no one loves them, yet it's not true. During adolescence young people often feel that their parents don't love them when it's not so. It is absolutely true that we all need to feel love and support. We need someone or several someones who care about us.

Frederick II, emperor of the Holy Roman Empire in the thirteenth century, was an eccentric kind of guy. Curious about what language was spoken by Adam and Eve in the Garden of Eden, he tried an experiment. He isolated a group of infants when they were born. Frederick's plan was that eventually, when the babies started communicating with each other, they would speak in their innate language and he would have his curiosity satisfied. He had them taken from their mothers and given to nurses who were issued instructions not to speak at all in the presence of these babies or even touch them except when it was absolutely necessary. An interesting experiment. There was only one thing wrong with it. Within a short period of time, every one of those babies died. Humans cannot thrive without others who love and support them.

How did Elijah finally recover from his weariness? First, he was helped by the resting of his body. Also, he was helped by the lifting of his sense of depression. In addition, he was helped by learning that he was not alone. But Elijah was made well by a spiritual experience on Mount Sinai, the holy mountain. This is what the biblical passage says happened: *There was a furious wind that split the rock and shattered the hill. But the Lord was not in the wind. And out of the wind there was an earthquake, but the Lord was not in the earthquake. And after the earthquake, there was a fire, but the Lord was not in the fire. And after the fire, there was the soft whisper of a voice* (I King 19:11,12).

How very much like our experience. Usually the times when we feel tired, depressed, and alone are times when our spiritual resources have been depleted. Remember that it was right after the greatest spiritual victory that Elijah felt his debilitating weariness. Life is so noisy. Our troubles shatter us. Our tasks weary us. Our bodies betray us. Our emotions overwhelm us. But there's a place, a place at the center of our existence, like Elijah's holy mountain, where we can still hear a soft whisper of a voice. It is the holy voice of God which speaks to our spirit.

> There is a place of quiet rest,
> near to the heart of God;
> A place where sin cannot molest,
> near to the heart of God.
> O Jesus, blest Redeemer,
> sent from the heart of God,
> Hold us who wait before thee
> near to the heart of God.
>
> Cleland B. McAfee

Today is the day you can overcome your fatigue and put it away for all time. Take time to rest. Claim the power of a positive attitude. Find purpose in your life. Seek out the people who love and support you. And listen—through the furious winds, the earthquakes, the fires of life—for that still, small voice of God, which speaks to our spirits.

Overcoming Adversity

John 16:33; Romans 5:1-5

I think about the times my community, located on the Gulf Coast, has focused on a hurricane. All the people look at the storm on the television screen, read about it in the newspapers, hear about it from neighbors, think about it, and hope it won't come this way. We are greatly relieved when it doesn't hit our town, and yet we recognize at the same time that when a hurricane doesn't come here, it goes somewhere else. When we are spared, others may not be.

That's true of hurricanes in nature and it's also true of other kinds, ones related to job stress, health, finances, marriages, children. There are all kinds of ways in which life twists itself around and blows hard and wreaks destruction. If those things aren't happening to us, they are happening to other people we know.

Jesus was right when he told us that the world will make us suffer: *In the world you will have trouble* (John 16:33 NIV).

Now it seems to me that there are different ways that one may respond to trouble. One I identify as *escape*. I don't mean being able to avoid trouble. If we are able to avoid it, we are going to do that. None of us wants to suffer, but when suffering inevitably comes, there are some who choose to try to run from it, to pretend that it's not there. And that reaction is quite unhealthy.

Drugs and alcohol are a retreat for many people who attempt to escape from the difficulties they face. Depression is an emotional retreat from adversity. Sometimes people pull away from family and friends. Sometimes they pull away from the church. I find it ironic that many persons, when life is hardest, turn away from those very resources that would enable them to face their difficulties. Much more important than what happens to us is the way we respond to those events.

In 1940, on the verge of Warld War II, western Europe was its bleakest. Holland had been overrun by the Nazis. So had Belgium. France had given up without a fight, and the British troops had been pushed to the sea at Dunkirk. At that point Winston Churchill called a meeting of his top advisors at Number Ten Downing Street, a gathering of frightened men in a frightening world situation. It is said that Churchill stood, looked every one of those men squarely in their frightened eyes, and said, "Gentlemen, I must say to you that I find this all terribly inspiring."

A far better way than to try to escape is to deal with the situation that confronts us. Years ago I came across a little saying about one of my heroes, a phrase that has stuck with me and has seen me through difficulty after difficulty: "The best way out is through." It's true always. The best way out is through.

Wilma Rudolph was born and brought up in a little shack in the backwoods of Tennessee, the child of a sharecropper family. Four-year-old Wilma was stricken with double pneumonia and scarlet fever and her left leg became paralyzed. People in her family's church prayed for the instantaneous and miraculous healing of that leg, but it did not come. Still Wilma Rudolph's mother did not despair. She said to this rail-thin little girl, "Wilma, don't ever give up. Trust God, and don't give up."

By the time she was nine, Wilma was able to discard the brace she had worn on her leg. By the age of thirteen she had gained enough confidence to attempt to run a junior high school race. She finished dead last. But in the 1960 Olympics Wilma Rudolph ran in both the 400-meter women's relay and in the showcase event of track and field, the 100-meter race. And she won gold medals.

Later as she faced the press she was asked, "How did you do it?"

She replied, "When I was four years old I knew I would be paralyzed for the rest of my life unless I was determined not to be. You see, it was not my ability that won; it was my determination."

For most of us determination eventually wears thin, and we find it difficult to look beyond the present problems to what can be beyond. A popular comic strip features Cathy, a young woman who has to deal with her own insecurities and lacks the determination to move forward in her life.

One sequence shows Cathy, on the telephone, seated on the couch with a friend, who is reading the newspaper. When Cathy puts down the telephone, she says to her friend, "That was Karen. Her boyfriend dumped her. She got mad, started her own business and just grossed $500,000 in sales." She goes on, "Joan went to Hawaii to recover from being fired. Landed a real estate deal and now is managing her own string of condominiums on the beach. Paula got fat, founded a weight loss clinic, lost fifty-three pounds and fell in love with the most handsome man I've ever seen in my life." And Cathy concludes, "Everyone I know is having a more productive crisis than I am."

Cathy's friends evidently were able to catch a vision of what could be, and when crisis arrived they took advantage of the opportunity. Often, however, our biggest hindrance is fear of an uncertain future.

Bishop Woody White tells about the time he received a telephone call from his distraught sister, reporting that something had happened to their mother. Although he was a couple of hundred miles away from the town where she lived, he raced to his car and drove as fast as he could, his mind whirling with questions and his stomach churning with fear. When he pulled in the driveway of his mother's house and dashed inside, he discovered that his seventy-three-year-old mother had been robbed, beaten, and raped. She was swollen and bruised and some of her wounds were still bleeding. Woody stood there in shock and then tenderly took her in his arms and began to cry.

Soon he became aware of a familiar fragrance from the kitchen, and he said, "Mama, what's that I smell?"

She said, "It's fried chicken, Son. I thought you might be hungry after your long drive."

Overcome with that beauty of spirit in the face of what had happened to her, he broke into tears again. She took his face in her hands, and said, "Son, I want to tell you something and I don't want you to ever forget it. God is still good, God is good, God is good."

When life gets hardest, I am most aware of my own weakness. And so it is very comforting to me that after Jesus said, *"In the world you will have trouble . . . ,"* he added *" . . . , but take heart! I have overcome the world"* (John 16:33 NIV). The secret is to look beyond your own strength to the strength of eternity. To claim the resources of heaven and earth so that you may rise above your own adversity.

When Paul wrote to the Romans, he said, We belong to Christ. His declaration means something for us for the life to come, but it also means something for us in our present circumstance, even if it's difficult—especially if it's difficult! Then Paul gives a three-step formula for moving from suffering to meaning, for moving from trouble to the place where we have a grip upon the circumstances of our lives.

Paul says, *Trouble brings endurance, and endurance wins God's approval, and God's approval produces hope, and hope will not disappoint us because God's love is poured out for us* (Romans 5:3-5).

When Christopher Columbus was crossing the Atlantic, not knowing exactly where he was going, it's said that every day in his log he made the same entry. He wrote, "This day we sailed on." No doubt some of the times when Columbus made that entry he was near despair himself. Storms battered the ships, the crew suffered from diseases, and they threatened mutiny. Every day there was just water and more water out there, water and water, no land, and day after day after day Columbus made his entry, "This day we sailed on."

When hardship comes into your life and mine, we are tempted to let up or to give up, but if we follow Paul's advice we can say, like Columbus, "This day I will sail on." Persons with addictive illnesses are taught to combat them one day at a time. It's the same with any kind of hardship. You can endure today.

A first grade teacher walked into the classroom to find Samuel, six years old, standing up in front of the class, straining to poke his stomach way out. To the teacher's puzzled look, he replied, "I had a tummy ache this morning and the school nurse said, "If you'll just stick it out till noon I think everything will be okay." We can all stick it out for just a little while.

"Trouble," Paul says, "produces endurance," and then he says a second thing. "Endurance then wins God's approval." Another way to say it is that endurance leads us to the place where we understand God's presence in the event. Now that's not the same as saying God causes the event. It's saying that somehow God will show us his approval and give us hope in our difficulty.

There was a breeder of horses in China whose prize stallion ran away into the hills. The villagers came to his house and expressed their regret that he had lost the source of his livelihood.

The man's response was, "Good or bad. Who's to say?"

In a matter of days, his prize stallion returned from the hills. Not only did the horse come back, but he brought some wild horses from the hills with him.

The villagers ran out to congratulate him: "Not only do you have your stallion back, but you have all these other horses, as well! You're even richer than you've been before. This is wonderful!"

The man gave the same response, "Good or bad. Who's to say?"

That very afternoon the rancher's son, riding to break one of those wild horses, was thrown from the horse and his leg was broken. The villagers came out again to express their regrets.

He said, "Good or bad—who's to say?"

When war broke out between that province and the neighboring one, all the healthy young men were conscripted for military service. But of course the rancher's son, with a broken leg, didn't go to war. And all the villagers came out . . . .

Well, the story goes on and on, but that's far enough to make the point. It says that in any given event, we cannot always understand the meaning. It's only in retrospect, only when we have God's perspective and look down upon that event (back, in our case), that we can see the imprint of his hand and we can see how he was guiding us.

Paul reminds us that God's approval produces hope. There is a gospel song that says much the same thing.

Oft' times the way is dreary,
  and rugged seems the road.
Oft' times I'm weak and weary
  when bent beneath some load.
But when I cry in weakness,
  How long, oh Lord, how long?"
Then Jesus takes my burden
  and leaves me with a song.

The poet does not intend to say that Jesus took the problem away. He is saying he took the *burden* of the problem away. Very often in our lives God calms the terrible storm around us, but there are those times when the storm continues to rage and God calms *us* in the midst of the storm.

Paul says that when we see God's sustaining hand finally, God's approval creates hope. Paul is saying to us that when life is hard, in the course of our enduring we discover that God is with us to sustain us.

The assurance of God's presence creates hope, and hope won't disappoint us. When you're troubled, you can look down the road to the victory that God is preparing for you, even though you may not know what it is. And you may trust him in it, understanding that he is present with you this day as you struggle to overcome adversity.

Overcoming Stress
Proverbs 17:22; Matthew 6:34; I Peter 5:6-7

I have been told that Americans consume ninety-seven percent of the world's aspirin. Rather an alarming statistic, don't you think? I don't know where we stand with
>Zantac,
>>Pepcid AC,
>>>Rolaids,
>>>>Sominex,
>>>>>Pepto Bismol
>>>>>>and Alka-Seltzer,

but their use is probably right up there, as well. I can't verify the accuracy of that statistic, but I can tell you this: we are a stressed society. One man said, "I have two fears. My first fear is that if I don't slow down I'm going to have a heart attack. And my second fear is that if I don't speed up I won't get enough done before I have my heart attack."

Some people are so tense they are about to become past-tense. And life continues to get more and more complex—to move faster and faster. Stress is an everyday factor for many people, and it's an occasional factor for so many others that virtually no one is untouched by it. It doesn't matter if you are a homemaker, the CEO of a company, a school teacher, a military person, or a student, there is stress in your life.

A major source of our stress is the workplace. Peter Drucker, the author of many books on management, predicted the increase in stress levels now being experienced.

> Businesses will undergo more radical restructuring in the 1990's than at any time since the modern corporate organization first evolved in the 1920's. These demands and changes add to each of us the need to keep our motivation high and to understand stress. In other words, it's bad out there in the work place. It's stressful, and it's going to get worse.

Another place where stress germinates is in the relationships we experience at home. There are some homes that are almost tension free, but there are far more homes where there is so much tension in the life of every individual that they can barely manage. That's almost always true where there are problems in the marriage, with young children, or with teenagers acting out. The problem is compounded where there are learning disabilities or handicapping conditions, where there are blended families, where some one person or several in a family have a substance abuse problem or if persons in that home are stressed at work or in other places.

Another source of stress in the lives of most people is money. I heard someone say, and I think it's a fair statement, that most people don't have a money problem, they have a management problem. Now there are, of course, people who don't have enough money to put bread on the table, but there are far more people who are in difficulty with their finances because they don't manage their incomes well. Whatever the case, twenty-nine years of marriage counseling has taught me that when families fight, very often it will be over money.

Another source of stress is health. This presents a double bind, because a vicious cycle is created. Health problems cause stress, and stress is likely to bring on additional health problems.

What do we do about the problem of stress? What is the Christian solution? What does the Bible have to say about stress to help us cope with it?

A lot! Three passages of scripture—one from the Old Testament, one from the Gospels, and one from the Epistles—have been very instructive for me.

In the book of Proverbs: *Being cheerful keeps you healthy. It is a slow death to be gloomy all the time.* Lighten it up. Don't take yourself and your concerns quite so seriously. In other words, if you can laugh with people and at yourself, you can relieve a great deal of stress.

One of the most popular politicians of this century was Hubert Humphrey, Senator from Minnesota and Vice President of the United States. Not everybody liked his politics, but everybody who knew him liked him personally. He was an enjoyable, happy, out-going kind of person. Once, when he was giving a speech on the campaign trail, there was a heckler in the audience who threw an over-ripe tomato which struck the Senator on his shoulder. The big glob of red goo ran on his shirt and tie and then fell to the ground. The crowd gasped, but Humphrey was undaunted. He said, "and speaking of agriculture . . . " then went on with his speech, to thunderous applause and a standing ovation.

General Omar Bradley told about an encounter on a commercial flight. He got on the airplane dressed in a business suit, rather than his usual military uniform. With a long flight ahead, he intended to do a lot of work. He sat down in an aisle seat next to an Army private in uniform. Not recognizing General Bradley, the young man turned to him and said, "Well, if we're going to be traveling for a long time, we need to get to know each other." Bradley, in a stern voice, replied, "I am General Bradley. General Omar Bradley. Five-star General Omar Bradley of the United States Army. Chairman of the Joint Chiefs of Staff at the Pentagon in Washington, D.C."

The private was silent for a moment. Then he furrowed his brow and said, "Well, sir, I sure hope you don't blow it."

Don't take yourself so seriously. In my own life I have found that many of the things that stress me are things that don't matter at all in the long run.

Some would-be poet said,

> "Don't make tragedies of trifles.
> Don't shoot butterflies with rifles."

The scripture in Proverbs is giving us important advice: *Lighten It Up.*

The scripture in Matthew says a second thing: *Break It Up.* Take those things which create stress in your life and chop them up in manageable segments so that your time and energy can remain focused. Jesus says it like this. *"Don't worry about tomorrow. There is no need to add to the trouble each day brings."* Jesus is not saying, don't plan for retirement, don't have life insurance. He's saying, don't worry. Don't take on, in this moment, all those problems you can't solve but deal with what's on your plate right now. Focus on that because it is manageable. That is stress which you can handle.

I can think of some commonly used items that tend to intensify stress. I'm as guilty as anyone I know of being a slave to the clock and the calendar and the schedule. Psalm 23 has been rewritten in a way that reflects the problem:

> The clock is my dictator, I shall not rest.
> It makes me lie down only when I am exhausted.
> It leads me into great depression.
> It hounds my soul.
> It leads me in circles of frenzy for activities' sake.
> Even though I run frantically from task to task,
> I'll never get it all done.
> For my ideal is with me.
> Deadlines and needs for approval, they drive me.
> They demand performance from me
>   beyond the limits of my schedule.
> They anoint my head with migraines.
> My in-basket overflows.
> Surely fatigue and time pressures shall follow me
>   all the days of my life;
> And I will dwell in the bonds of frustration forever.

Every one of us needs time away from time. We need those occasions when there is no schedule at all. Sometimes when people learn that I enjoy playing golf, they comment: "Well I don't play golf, it takes too long." And my reply is standard: "That's exactly why I play it. Because it takes a long time. Because it takes long enough that whatever stress has built up in me is dissipated by the time the game is over." There's only one place I don't take my watch and that's on the golf course. I never think about time out there.

Whatever it is that releases stress for you—whether it's on a boat or with your paints and easel or at your workbench or on your volunteer job somewhere—you need a place and a period of time when you are not concerned about schedules and about time. It needs to be long enough that you can break up that tension.

Another instrument that very often works against us is the telephone. And now, thanks to call-waiting, you can be engaged in a stressful conversation which you can put on hold while you take another stressful telephone call. You can actually be stressed by two conversations simultaneously!

Try to remember that you are not there for the phone; the phone is there for you. Particularly is this true at home. When the phone rings, you don't have to answer it. If it rings while you're having dinner or praying or reading your Bible or engaged in a meaningful conversation, I promise that if you don't answer it, it will stop ringing. Use the clock and the phone to make your life less stressful and more productive. Don't let them drive you. Take a break.

The Bible has one more bit of advice for us: *Give It Up*. The writer of First Peter says, God will lift you in his time. Leave all your worries with him because he cares for you. Flipping television channels one day I saw a program about a famous fortress in Austria. It hangs on the side of a mountain, a mighty fortress overlooking the charming city of Salzburg. As I watched, I could envision those huge cannon balls bouncing off the wall of that fortress. Arrows. Spears. I thought then about the great reformer Martin Luther. Nobody in history had more to deal with than Luther did in 1529 when he had the Pope and the Roman Catholic Church and the Holy Roman Empire all on his neck. As I saw this television program, I thought about Luther and his enemies, firing their theological cannons at each other. Nothing could harm Luther because his God was "a mighty fortress . . ., a bulwark never failing."

Your strength and mine will run out, but there is available to us eternal power, eternal resources. God himself will hold you up and lift you up if you will give up to him that which is your concern.

Bruce Larson, the author/pastor, has done a great deal of pastoral counseling. He said that in New York he often had businessmen who came to him for help when they were so stressed out from their work they could barely cope. Larson said that very often he would say, "Let's take a field trip." They would go down the elevator, out the door and down Fifth Avenue to the RCA building and Rockefeller Center. Overlooking the ice rink there is a statue of Atlas, massive, muscular, and powerful. Resting on his shoulders is planet earth. As strong as Atlas is, it is obvious that he can barely hold up the weight of the whole world on his shoulders. Larson said, "We would stand there for a while and then I would point to the statue and say, "That's one way you can live your life."

Then they would walk across Fifth Avenue to St. Patrick's Cathedral. Inside that holy place, down the center aisle and near the main altar is a statue of the boy Jesus, maybe eight or nine years old. Jesus is holding, quite easily, the world in his hands.

A spiritual from the days of slavery captures the truth expressed in that small shrine.

> He's got the whole world in his hands.
> He's got the little bitty baby in his hands.
> He's got you and me, Brother, in his hands,
> He's got you and me, Sister, in his hands,
> He's got the whole world in his hands.

Overcoming Stress

It can be true for you if you intentionally place yourself and your concerns in his hands and give them up to him. The troubles of yesterday may still be with you, but yesterday is gone. The hope of tomorrow is still only a hope. Today is the only day you have to turn your stress over to Almighty God.

Overcoming Temptation
Hebrews 2:17-18

A pastor I know went to preach at a small church in Alabama. Standing at the pulpit to give the sermon, he found there two notes which had apparently been left by someone attempting to be helpful to the preacher. One of those notes was a copy of The Lord's Prayer. The other note was about the public address system in that church. It said, "Speak directly into the microphone. The agnostics in here are terrible."

At my church we don't have a problem with agnostics in the sanctuary, but we do have a problem—every one of us—with temptation.

Temptation is inevitable. It is not inevitable that we sin, but it is inevitable that we are tempted. Do you remember the highly controversial film, The *Last Temptation of Christ?* It seems to me that much of the uproar about that movie came because we didn't want to

77

think that Jesus was tempted the way we are. Yet the Bible says that he was tempted in every way that we are. It also says that he did not sin (Hebrews 4:15). Now if it is true that Jesus was tempted, it is far more true of us. In order to understand how we might avoid temptation, I think it's important to look at some of the subtle forms temptation takes.

I think, for instance, that we are tempted by the impulse to resist rules. I have a son, Bert, now in his mid-thirties, of whom I'm very proud. But there was a time in his teenage years when he struggled quite a bit. As a result of his struggles I, as his father, struggled quite a bit, too. That was a difficult period for both of us. But the relationship which was so strained in those years has been restored beautifully.

Not long ago he said to me, "Back then, if you said 'don't do it,' that made me want to do it."

"What happened to love? What happened to obedience? Why would you want to do it just because I said 'don't do it'?" I asked.

He said, "I don't know, but I did."

I've thought about that a lot and I've come to realize that it's human nature. In one of the earliest stories of the Bible we are told about the temptation of Adam and Eve.

Overcoming Temptation

God, the authority, said, "Have all the peaches you want, and get some of those strawberries—they're especially good—and take some oranges and tangerines and kiwi fruit. Have anything you want, except don't eat an apple." So what did Adam and Eve do? Their desire for their own experience caused them to be tempted.

Sometimes temptation comes in the form of wanting to resist whatever is a rule. That doesn't mean, of course, that there shouldn't be rules. It means that we have to learn to trust that the rules are in our best interest.

Another form which temptation takes is the tendency to choose the short-run over the long-run. The tendency to choose what we want now rather than what is best for the future. Let's say you want to lose twenty pounds. You begin a diet, eating broiled fish, romaine lettuce, carrot sticks, and parsley. On the next trip to the grocery store, you pass the refrigerated case that has Dove Bars in it. You begin salivating at the thought of incredible ice cream covered by even more incredibly rich dark Belgium chocolate. What do you do? If you choose the short-run, you satisfy yourself at the time but you punish yourself in terms of the real goal that you want to reach.

An old-time Methodist preacher used to say, "Don't sacrifice the permanent on the altar of the immediate."

Temptation always shows us its best facade immediately. But it is like the scenes in the western movies I used to watch when I was a kid. Gene Autry or Roy Rogers would ride into some cowboy town with a saloon and a hotel and a livery stable. But not really. Behind the set, scaffolds were propping up the fronts. Each building was simply a false front.

In 1787 when Catherine the Great planned a journey across Russia, the great Russian statesman Potemkin preceded her, making arrangements so that she would see only beauty and happiness. Henri Troyat has described the trip in his book *Catherine the Great*:

> They sailed down the Dnieper slowly and magnificently. Orchestras played lively airs on the flag-bedecked galleys. The facades of the houses were decorated with garlands and carpets. Everything was smiling, welcoming and prosperous. There were only happy people in Russia; not one dilapidated hovel, not one ragged beggar. Individuals of unprepossessing appearance were driven well inland, and huts on the verge of collapse were hidden behind light structures of painted wood. These were the "Potemkin villages" that caused the Prince de Ligne to wonder if they had roofs, doors,

windows or inhabitants. During the night crews of workers laid out roads that would be used only once, gardens destined for a single glance. "Once the empress had passed," wrote the Comte de Langeron, "all these unfortunates were driven back to their homes. Many died from the consequences of this transplantation."

Evil shows us its best face, but behind that face there is nothing of value. Temptation comes to us in this form and it invites us to choose the now and to reject what is right and good and best for the long haul.

Temptation also comes in the belief that we can trust our feelings. Many times we get into trouble because we believe that we can trust what we feel.

A trucker who drove an eighteen-wheeler pulled in late one night at a truck stop in Broken Bow, Nebraska. He went inside, placed his order, and was minding his own business. In the door came three bikers, motorcycle gang guys, the kind who ride those huge motorcycles sometimes called "hogs."

One biker picked up the truck driver's hamburger and took a bite out of it. Another grabbed a handful of his french fries and ate them. The third guy grabbed his cup of coffee and downed it.

But the trucker didn't respond the way they expected. He simply stood up, left the tip on the table, went to the cashier and paid for his food. She watched him as he walked out the door, got in his truck and drove off. As she watched his truck disappear down the road, one of the bikers came up and said, "He ain't much of a man, is he?"

She said, "No, and he ain't much of a truck driver, either. He just ran over three motorcycles out in the parking lot."

Put yourself in that guy's place. Doesn't that feel good? But sometimes when we choose what we feel, what happens is destructive. Our feelings can lie to us. Our feelings can tell us something is okay when it's not okay. So what do we do to resist that temptation? We have to learn to trust the rules and not our feelings.

The remedy for temptation and for afterwards, when we have given in to temptation, is the truth that Christ is our guardian. Jesus became like us in order to be in every respect a merciful and faithful high priest in the service of God, to help us with our temptations and to forgive us.

Jesus became like his brothers and sisters so that he might make a sacrifice of atonement for the sins of the people. Because he himself was tested by what he suffered, he is able to help those who are being tested (Hebrews 2:17,18).

When I was a small boy I very often would go visit my grandparents in the little town of Whatley, Alabama. Whatley is so small that the *Welcome to Whatley* and *Resume Speed* messages are on the same sign. Well, almost. All the sights of Whatley were concentrated down at the end of Main Street, which terminated at the railroad track. My brother and my cousins and I would go down to the train station to see the passenger train stop in the mornings on the way toward Mobile and in the afternoons on the way back. Sometimes someone would get off or someone would get on.

The cotton gin was down there. My grandfather ran the cotton gin, so my brother and my cousins and I were sometimes allowed to play on the bales of cotton. We liked even more to get into the big barn-like area into which the cottonseed were blown and play on the cottonseed.

Also at the end of Main Street was Mr. Udell's store, the only place in town we could get ice cream. In those pre-air-conditioning days on a hot July afternoon there was nothing quite so wonderful as getting a nickel from my grandmother and going down to Mr. Udell's to buy a cup of ice cream. We would very carefully take the top off the container and lick the inside of the lid to expose the picture of Roy Rogers or Jane Russell or Mickey Mantle. And we would eat the ice cream slowly with a wooden spoon.

There was also in that vicinity what we called the Overflowing Well. It was an artesian well, from an underground spring. Someone had installed an L-shaped pipe so that the water flowed out of it, cold and clear and pure. They had drilled a quarter-inch hole in the top of the pipe so that putting a hand over the end of the pipe would force the water up out of the hole in a six- or eight-inch stream. A kid could create his own water fountain. The water bubbled up, the coldest and purest and best I've ever tasted.

I hadn't been to the well for maybe thirty years. The years had passed and I sort of forgot about the places I had loved. But a few years ago on an autumn day I turned off Highway 84 and went down to the foot of Main Street. The railroad station is gone. The passenger trains don't run anymore, just an occasional freight train that zooms past. The cotton gin has long since ceased to be used. The roof is caved in and there're still some boards sticking up, but the spot is now grown over in

Overcoming Temptation

weeds and even trees. Mr. Udell's store is not there, either.

But I found the Overflowing Well. There it was, the pipe, the stream still flowing. I knelt down in the gravel and put my hand at the end of the pipe and the water bubbled up for me! Still cold, still pure, still clean. I found myself thinking about all the years I didn't visit there. I probably hadn't even thought of that place in twenty years. And all the while, all the days and nights, that water was flowing, pure and clean. Every day and every night for whoever needed refreshment, whoever would stop and receive what it had to offer. And I thought of another well, where Jesus met a woman and said to her, *Whoever drinks of the water I will give you will never thirst. The water I shall give you will become a spring of water welling up to eternal life.*

I don't know where *your* attention has been through the years. I just want you to know that if you've given in to temptation here and there—perhaps even more often—there is still a source of nourishment to help you resist. There is a source of cleansing. It is life-giving water, provided by Christ our guardian. Today is the day for you to drink of that water.

Practicing Perseverance

Psalm 131:1-2; Galatians 6:9

Henry VIII was one of the most notorious British monarchs of all time. He was famous for his excesses: for his girth, for his appetite, for the number of his wives and for his varied and unique rationales for disposing of them. For many years it was believed that Henry VIII died because he ate too much or he contracted venereal disease. A researcher discovered recently that Henry VIII died because he did not eat a balanced diet. He ate huge amounts but, for the most part, only meats. As a result of this lack of fruits and vegetables he developed scurvy and he died.

Balance is necessary, not just in diet but in all areas of life, including the spiritual life. Balance is tricky, however. Some qualities we strive for may even appear, at first glance, to be contradictory. In fact, when considered together, they form the kind of balance necessary to live a life that is good and right. One pair of such qualities is perseverance and contentment.

I don't suppose there is any quality that is any more admired than perseverance. Almost daily, certainly every week, the news is full of stories of persons who overcome tremendous obstacles and achieve great ends because they persevere. They don't give up! Just recently there was a news story about an amputee who climbed to the top of a great high mountain. That's perseverance!

Perseverance pays in less dramatic ways, as well. When the Coca-Cola Company first began to market its product in the nation of China, company executives considered the difference in language and the nature of the Chinese characters and decided to use a phonetic version of its brand name, "Koo-Kah-Koo-Lah." The promotional people could not figure out why the sales were not good until finally they learned that "Koo-Kah-Koo-Lah," means literally translated, "bite the waxed tadpole." Sales rose dramatically when they began to call their product "Kah-Koo-Kah-Lah," which literally translated means, "may the happy mouth rejoice." Life is good when we make the appropriate adjustments after our failures.

Practicing Perseverance

Two sportscasters were talking about the greatest running back of all time, Walter Payton, who in the course of his career gained more than 16,000 yards—far, far more than any other player in NFL history. Trying to put that in perspective, one sportscaster said, "Do you realize that Walter Payton gained more than nine miles running the football?"

The other one came right back, "Yes, and he got knocked down every 4.6 yards of the way."

So we know that a part of Walter Payton's greatness was his ability to persevere. Greatness, you see, is not determined by whether or not we fall; it is determined by whether we get up and persevere.

There's not a single person anywhere who hasn't fallen. No matter who you are or how successful, somewhere along the line there's something you've tried to do and couldn't. Something you wanted to accomplish and just couldn't pull off. What do you do when that happens? The key to perseverance is a willingness to start over. It is a willingness to accept a temporary defeat, pick ourselves up, and allow the Holy Spirit to infuse us with a brand new power and energy. And we start again.

The Apostle Paul, encourages us: *So let us not grow weary in doing what is right, for we will reap at harvest-time, if we do not give up* (Galatians 6:9). This truth applies to our parenting, to our jobs, to all the worthy "works" we have undertaken. Work hard and don't quit, and when the time is right you will be rewarded.

Way out on the other side of perseverance is its counterbalance, contentment. Recently a *USA Today* poll asked people, "What do you want most in life?" The most frequent answer was peace of mind, contentment, the capacity to find tranquillity and serenity outside of continued effort and anxiety. Sometimes the appropriate adjustment means realizing that we have pushed far enough. Sometimes circumstance requires new goals. Sometimes a new insight dictates a new perspective. Sometime it is important to be able to say with the Psalmist:

O Lord, my heart is not lifted up,
my eyes are not raised too high;
I do not occupy myself with things
too great and too marvelous for me.
But I have calmed and quieted my soul,
like a weaned child with its mother;
my soul is like the weaned child that is with me.
                                        Psalms 131:1,2

Many years ago a very great man had experienced a variety of severe and painful physical difficulties. He'd been misunderstood and maligned and, as a result of those misunderstandings, had been jailed. Facing execution and enduring the hardships of prison, he wrote an unforgettable and oft-quoted letter which contained these words: "... *for I have learned to be content with whatever I have.*" That lesson learned is how the Apostle Paul was able to deal with life.

We seek a balance between persisting and being content with where we are, regardless of what is going on around us. Just as the Bible speaks of giving our best, so it speaks of being still. The Bible speaks of hard work and struggle, but it also speaks of contemplation and a feeling of peace.

I personally lean toward the perseverance side and sometimes find myself beating a dead horse. I need some work on the contentment side, on quieting and calming my soul. I know how necessary it is to be able to find tranquillity when I've done all I can do. Knowing it and experiencing it are two different things.

In 1934, in the little village of Heath, Massachusetts, the small Congregational Church invited the noted theologian Reinhold Niebuhr, a summer resident of

Today is the Only Day!

that village, to preach one Sunday morning. He was sitting in the pulpit chair, waiting to begin, when he realized that he would want to offer a brief prayer at the end of the sermon, so on the worship service bulletin for the morning he jotted down a short and simple prayer. He preached a well-prepared and thoughtful, theologically sensitive discourse and prayed the little prayer he had written. In the congregation was another person of some renown, Howard Chandler Robbins, the Dean of the Cathedral of St. John the Divine in New York City, one of the largest cathedrals in the world and an influential congregation. At the end of the service Robbins said not a word about the sermon but asked if he could have a copy of that little prayer. He printed it in his own church newsletter, and from there it was picked up by others elsewhere. Today that little prayer is one of the most widely known and prayed Christian prayers in the world. We know it as "The Serenity Prayer."

> God, grant me the serenity
> to accept the things I cannot change,
> the courage to change the things I can,
> and the wisdom to know the difference.

In that prayer and in that truth lies the proper balance between perseverance and contentment. Today is the day to begin to seek and practice that balance.

Practicing Patience
Matthew 25:1-13

If you've ever been to a wedding, you know what it means to wait. First, you wait in the church. They seat you as early as they can and you wait while some well-dressed usher escorts the grandmamas and the mamas. Then some pretty young lady sings a sweet, romantic, contemporary song which has little to do with what you are there for. But it makes the bride's and groom's hearts go pitter-pat. And then maybe she sings something like, "Sunrise, Sunset," from *Fiddler On The Roof*,

> Where is the little girl I carried?
> Where is the little boy at play?
> I don't remember growing older,
> When did they?

Then the mamas and daddys start to cry.

Afterwards, you wait at the reception, while the wedding party is having pictures made in the church.

You stand around getting hungry, looking at all that good food. Then you wait after the reception, outside, because they give you some rice or—more commonly now—bird seed to throw, and finally you line up on either side and the bride and groom come out and you throw bird seed on each other because the bride and groom duck.

If you've ever presided as the minister at a wedding, you really know what it means to wait. You wait the night before at the rehearsal because everybody in the wedding party is hyper, they get there late, and some groomsman has gone to the wrong church. Before the wedding you wait for the ceremony to start. It's usually my responsibility to look after the groom and the best man. So we wait in my office. I don't know what is going on with the bride or even where she is. But I do know what is going on with the groom. He's looking in the mirror and recombing his hair for the forty-third time. Or he's pacing back and forth across my office. Or he's asking the best man again, "Are you sure you've got the ring?" Or if, as is sometimes the case, the father of the groom is the best man, he's saying, "Son, remember this!" and giving some totally useless advice at the last moment.

After the ceremony you wait for the pictures to be made. The photographer has to change the film in his camera or his flash doesn't go off or the little ring bearer won't be still.

Weddings have always involved waiting and they have always involved preparation. That's why almost two thousand years ago, when Jesus wanted to tell a story to make this point about waiting, he set the story at a wedding. His stories, or parables, were often his way of preaching. Somehow those who heard him heard in those stories their own story and the truth about their lives.

This particular story Jesus told is about ten bridesmaids. It is a big wedding. The bride and groom have been delayed at the church—no doubt taking pictures—and the bridesmaids have gone on to the reception. The custom in that time was that the bridesmaids carried lamps, or lanterns, which were fueled by oil. Five of these bridesmaids are wise; they are prepared and have brought extra oil. Five of them are otherwise; they haven't prepared and brought extra oil. Then when the word gets to the reception that the limo has left the church with the bride and groom, the five foolish girls look at their lamps and discover they don't have enough oil. And so they say to the other five, "You've got extra oil. Share it with us." But those five say, "We don't have enough for everybody. You should have gotten extra oil while we were waiting around. You'll have to go the Seven-Eleven store and get some." So the five foolish girls go to the store. While they are gone the bride and groom arrive, the reception begins and the food gets served. When the five bridesmaids return, the door has been locked. They have missed the party.

That's the story. Very obviously about waiting. About what happens when we want or need something and expect it to be provided for us. What is the truth for our lives when we have to wait, when we can't have immediately what we want or need?

The first truth is, have patience. We have to learn to be patient. I'm not very good at patience. I can't stand to stand in line. I can't stand to wait in traffic. I have this feeling that every traffic light owes it to me to be green when I get to it. Driving across the bay bridge when traffic is heavy, I almost invariably get behind a van or a bus or a truck, so I can't see. And I can't stand not to be able to see where I am going. I want a car with a periscope. I'm not naturally patient, so I have to concentrate on practicing patience.

We've all been admonished to be patient while we are waiting for good things to happen, but it's especially important to be patient when we are waiting out the worst. There is an illness—yours, or someone you love. Or there is a betrayal—your beloved has been unfaithful to you. Or your child is doing drugs or failing at school. In these or similar instances there are certain things you can do, but you can't solve the problem immediately. You must be patient and wait.

One of the questions people most often ask me, when there is a great problem, is "Why doesn't God do something?" My answer often is "God is doing something, but He is also asking you to do something. He is asking you to hold on and wait."

Some years ago four crewmen on the commercial fishing boat, *Can Do*, got into trouble in the waters off the coast of Charleston, South Carolina. Greg Palmer, one of those four crewmen, said, "It must have taken a bad wave. The boat filled up quick."

Of the four, Stacy Chancy, of Jacksonville, didn't make it from the boat to the raft when the boat went down. Tommy Waters, of Georgia, died soon after, apparently from drinking too much salt water. But the other two, Greg Palmer of Raleigh, North Carolina, and Robert Louis Watson of Pensacola, Florida, prayed and waited from four o'clock Sunday morning, all day Sunday and all that night and all day Monday and all that night. Then on Tuesday, after fifty-five hours of precarious survival in that raft, Robert Watson, twenty-seven years old, said, "I just can't take it any more" and rolled off the raft. One hour later, a Coast Guard jet spotted the raft and a Coast Guard helicopter rescued Greg Palmer.

Suppose Robert Watson had known that rescue was only an hour away. Do you think he would have held on? Of course he would. When we think we have to hold on forever, we cannot, but when we remember that we only have to hold on for an hour, we can. Nothing is more important than holding and keeping on, not giving up or giving in. When we are waiting out the worst, we have to be patient. Robert Louis Stevenson said, "Every man can endure until nightfall."

Every year at our local high school commencement exercises I am thrilled as I watch all of those splendid young people receive their diplomas. Each year I am especially thrilled as so many of our own church young people are honor graduates, and always two or three of them make speeches. Each year I recall the commencement address that Winston Churchill is said to have made, maybe the shortest ever given and certainly one of the most memorable. After he was

Practicing Patience

introduced, Churchill strode to the lectern and said eight words, "Never, never, never, never, never, never give up." Then he returned to his seat.

In his parable about the wise and otherwise, Jesus is saying to us that we have to be patient. But he also has another lesson: we don't just wait, we are to prepare and be ready for the time when the awaited circumstances, good or bad, come.

Remember the story about the Texas oil well that caught on fire? A $5,000 reward was offered. All the famous firefighters were called in to try to put out the fire. Even Red Adair, the most famous oil well-fire-putter-outer in the world, couldn't put the fire out. Then this little volunteer fire department, three guys in an old dilapidated fire truck, came wheeling in. They had three buckets of sand, two pails of water and a blanket. The old truck sped up to this raging inferno and disappeared right in the middle of that fire. The bystanders stood there gasping as those three guys jumped off that old truck, threw those two pails of water and three buckets of sand and the blanket on the fire, which promptly died! Everybody was amazed, overwhelmed. Afterwards a reporter asked, "What are you going to do with your $5,000 reward?"

The volunteer fireman said, "Well, we haven't talked about it yet, but I imagine we'll buy some new brakes for that fire truck."

Once in a while, you can get away with not being prepared, but not very often. Larry Bird, the new coach of the Indianapolis Pacers professional basketball team, was generally acknowledged by his peers and by others who know the game of basketball to rank with Michael Jordan as the greatest basketball player in the world. Bird twice won the award for the MVP in the NBA. By his own admission he couldn't run, and he couldn't jump, the two most important skills for a basketball player. Not only that, but he didn't shoot his jump shot correctly. He would fall away rather than going straight up and leaning in. Why was Larry Bird the greatest basketball player in the world before Michael Jordan? Because he prepared himself. Relentlessly.

Several years ago, the movie *Rocky* spawned a whole series of films about underdogs overcoming all obstacles. The most memorable scenes in the Rocky movies are not the fight sequences, which tend to run together, but the training sequences. It's Rocky running up the huge flat steps of that Memorial building in Philadelphia. It's Rocky running through the streets of Philadelphia with all those school children trailing behind him. It's Rocky and Apollo Creed racing on the beach. It's Rocky climbing to the top of a mountain in Siberia. It's Rocky, who has limited gifts, preparing himself.

Why are we so taken with preparation? Because most of us don't do enough of it. While we are waiting, we must use what God has given us to be ready for the moment God gives us when it comes.

The great contemporary preacher John Claypool tells about a time in his childhood when his father took him to the barber shop, where the shoeshine stand was operated by an enterprising old man. He wore overalls with a huge button on the right-hand side of the bib that trumpeted, "WHILE YOU WAIT." It was obviously a very effective bit of advertising because many of the men who went into that barber shop had their shoes shined while they waited to get their hair cut.

The young Claypool found out that the old gentleman was also a part-time Pentecostal preacher. On Sundays he preached the Gospel, and during the week he wore another button on the left-hand side of his overall bib which said, "JESUS SAVES."

Claypool said that one day he was sitting in the barber chair when he saw this old gentleman, really saw him, for the first time. Suddenly he saw this message: WHILE YOU WAIT, JESUS SAVES.

This is the message of Jesus' story about the wedding. The waiting we do can become worthwhile if we use that time to prepare ourselves for what is to come.

Patience is the name of the game. To practice patience today, as we prepare ourselves for tomorrow, can become a redemptive act. And today is the only day we have to begin.

Using What God Has Given

Matthew 25:14-30

There was a legendary fisherman down in Louisiana bayou country whose fame had spread. One day a stranger came to the fish camp and asked to go fishing with this man. As he got into the boat, the stranger noticed that the fisherman didn't have poles or a rod and reel. All he had in the dirty old boat were a net and a rusty old tackle box. When they finally reached a remote bayou where huge oak trees with tangles of Spanish moss hanging down to the water emphasized the quietness, the stranger watched with interest. The fisherman opened that old tackle box, pulled out a stick of dynamite, struck a match, lit the fuse, and flipped the dynamite overboard. There was the muffled sound of an explosion from the water and then a lot of dead fish rose to the surface. The fisherman took the net and raked the dead fish into the boat.

The stranger leaped up, flipped out a badge and said, "Ah, ha! I caught you! I'm the new game warden."

The old fisherman just calmly reached back into the tackle box, took another stick of dynamite, struck a match, lit the fuse, and handed the stick of dynamite to the startled game warden. Then he said, "Well, are you gonna fish, or are you just gonna sit there?"

Sometimes God says to us, "Are you gonna use that gift I gave you, or are you just gonna sit there?"

The story of the talents in Matthew 25 is about a man who had a great deal of money. When he went away for an extended vacation, he left his money in the hands of his three servants, to each according to his ability. The man who was given the equivalent of 5,000 silver coins invested in the stock market and he did well. In fact, he doubled his amount so that by the time the master returned he had 10,000 coins. The man who was given 2,000 silver coins invested in real estate, and he also did well. By the time the Master returned he had 4,000 silver coins. But the guy who had 1,000 coins, less than the others, was concerned that if he tried to invest, he might lose some of what he had. And so he poured those 1,000 silver coins in a large bag, went out into his backyard just off his porch, dug a hole, and buried the coins. When the Master returned, he praised the first two men and gave them more responsibility. But to the man who had been given the least, the Master said, "You bad and lazy person. You at least could have put the money in the bank and earned interest at the passbook savings rate. The person who has much will have even more, and the person who has very little will lose even what he has."

I used to think, how unfair. Jesus seems to be picking on the guy who had the least to begin with. But Jesus is not telling us how things ought to be; he's telling us how things are. And the truth is that if we use what we have, it tends to multiply, regardless of the amount of our gift. If we fail to use it, then we tend to lose it. It's a warning and it's an opportunity.

Now what are the story's truths for us? The first and the clearest is this: everybody received something. That fact is not what we tend to focus on. What we tend to focus on is that the gifts they received were unequal and that what they did with them was different. One of the ways that we deny our God-given gifts is by comparing what others have received to what we have. The man with the 1,000 silver coins was no doubt intimidated by the fact that one had 5,000. A "C" student, very often intimidated because he can't make A's or B's, doesn't try, and therefore he doesn't make C's either. He makes D's and F's. He's not using the talent, the gift that he was given.

It is deadly to compare ourselves with other people because we can always find those who have received more than we did, regardless of the gift. The young man who wants to grow up to be tall can look at Dikembe Mutombo (with the Atlanta Hawks basketball team), who is 7 feet, 2 inches tall. But even Dikembe Mutombo has to look up to Gheorghe Muresan (with the Washington Bullets basketball team), who is 7 feet, 7 inches tall. There's always somebody with more. Whatever you do in life there's somebody who does it better than you do. Don't compare yourself with others. Instead, compare yourself with your ideal self, with your best. Believe in your own gift and in the power of God implanted in you to let that gift be nurtured and grow.

One of the ways we do that is by the gift of imagination, the power of our minds to increase a gift or to see it diminish. A young ballplayer facing a good pitcher is afraid that he'll strike out. He's tentative. He's defensive. What is he thinking? He's thinking how he can avoid striking out. But the thought that is dominant is *striking out. How can I avoid striking out?* He is far more likely to do just that than the same ballplayer who comes to the plate thinking *line drive. I can hit this guy. I can hit the ball that's over the plate.* He's thinking positive. His mind is telling his body to succeed and success is far more likely to happen.

The parable of the talents teaches that you are gifted. But it also teaches that God is not satisfied unless you increase that gift. He is not satisfied if you return it to him exactly as you received it. You must do better with it.

There is another truth that the story teaches: to fail to use those gifts is to lose them. When I was still in grammar school I read that the fish in the underground caves at Mammoth Cave, Kentucky, have no eyes at all. Years and years ago, the fish there had eyes, but because it is so dark in those underground caves, they couldn't use their sight, and so over the course of years they've lost their eyes. If you tied your right arm down to your side for six months, you would discover that it had decreased in mobility and be far less useful than your left arm, which you would have been exercising all the time.

In this story God is challenging you and me to use what God has given us or we'll lose it.

Once your gifts are claimed and used, they multiply, and you discover you have new gifts that you never knew that you had. Norman Vincent Peale said, "Repeat ten times the words of Paul, 'I can do all things through Christ, who strengthens me' and you will discover it will change your life." I believe that. I can do all things through Christ, who strengthens me. If we believe that, the gifts we already know we have will become stronger and we discover that we have resources and talents we never dreamed we had. The negative destroys. The positive builds and even creates.

By all known laws which can be proven on paper or in the wind tunnel, the bumble bee cannot fly. The size of its wings in relation to its body, according to aeronautical and mechanical science, simply means that it cannot fly. But of course, the bumble bee doesn't know these rules, and so it goes ahead and flies anyway.

If you believe in your own gifts, even if those around you don't believe in them, you will discover that they multiply.

Carl Joseph grew up in Madison, Florida, a county-seat town of 3500 people east of Tallahassee. Carl was

Using What God Has Given

6 feet tall and weighed 180 pounds. He won thirteen letters in high school, in football, basketball, and track. He could dunk the basketball, quite a feat for a person who is only 6 feet tall. He could high jump 5 feet, 10 inches, and he was an outstanding linebacker on the football team. Now those are excellent achievements for an athlete but not really thought to be remarkable. Until you discover the special thing about this young man. Carl Joseph was born with only one leg.

During his senior year in high school the news about Carl Joseph began to get out. Bryant Gumble interviewed him on the *Today* program. He also appeared on the TV show, *That's Incredible*. Bart Starr, at that time head coach of the Green Bay Packers, had him flown to Green Bay to meet the team. The town of Madison had a Carl Joseph Day when he graduated. Many celebrities, mostly football coaches and professional athletes, came to speak and to honor this remarkable young man. When all the speeches had been made, they asked Carl if he would come forward and speak. So this shy young man took the microphone in his hand and stood on his one leg and said, "I'm not much of a talker, but my Mama taught me to pray, so let's all pray." And Carl Joseph began to pray for everybody. It was said that when he finished, there was not a dry eye in the place.

One of the people present for that occasion was Coach Jackie Sherrill, then the head coach at the University of Pittsburgh. And he gave Carl Joseph a full football scholarship, knowing full well that at 180 pounds, and with only one leg, the young man would never play a down for the University of Pittsburgh team. Why did Coach Sherrill give the scholarship anyway? Because he knew that this young man, with his indomitable spirit, would be an inspiration to all the players on his team. A couple of years later, Coach Sherrill resigned his position at Pittsburgh to take the head coaching job at Texas A&M, and when he did, Carl Joseph decided to come home to Florida and enroll at Bethune-Cookman College. In 1985, Carl Joseph played linebacker for the Bethune-Cookman football team, the only one-legged football player in America. He took what God gave him and used it and God multiplied it.

God will multiply your talents if you will use them. God isn't comparing your talents to anyone else's. So why should you? God simply expects you to use the power of your mind today to add to your gifts. So why not? Today is the only day you have!

Dealing With Difficult People
Matthew 5:38-44

Difficult people come in all shapes and sizes. One never knows when the mildly difficult person will become an explosively difficult person. Some mild-mannered persons collect and nurture their problems until they can't handle them any more.

I think of the quiet, hard-working father of four, who was a member of the school board and a Boy Scout leader. One morning he saw his wife off to work and his children off to school. Then he drove to the paper company where he worked. He shot nine colleagues, five of them supervisors who had been promoted over him. Then he drove to the airport and shot a switchboard operator who was a member of a carpool that had rejected him. He then drove back the short distance to his home in Loganton, Pennsylvania, walked across the street and shot his neighbors, still in bed. The neighbor had burned some leaves and the smoke had irritated him. By 9:30 a.m. the police had shot him and the next day he died. Before he expired, Leo Hale said, "I had had all I could take."

The incredible rage which sent this person on a rampage that killed six people and critically wounded six others appeared to be caused by a combination of rejection, hurt, envy, frustration, and disappointment. Perhaps those are the things that make difficult people difficult. Obviously, there was a desperate need for someone to listen and to care.

We all encounter them, difficult people, although hopefully not as difficult as Leo Hale. We don't even know such a person. Or do we? Who knows how many Leo Hales are walking time bombs, waiting for a spark to detonate them? Even if people aren't violent, they can be difficult and you and I still have to deal with them. At every age and station we encounter such people.

When I was a child, Noel Spinks lived across the street and up on the corner. Two years older, bigger, stronger—he was a bully! I would take the long way home from school just to keep from having to encounter him! I was afraid of Noel Spinks. In fact, when my parents announced that the Spinks family was moving to

South Florida, it was one of the happiest days of my life. But I still remember Noel and the difficulties he caused me.

When I was a young preacher I served quite a variety of little country churches. Every weekend I would drive out somewhere to hold worship services and serve my congregations. Many times I would preach several times on Sunday. I got to know and love the people even though, with maturity, I had begun to recognize that there were always difficult people around.

One of these people who seemed at the time to be very difficult attended one of those country churches. I didn't think she liked me—or my preaching. I'm still not certain. I took refuge in the thought that she didn't like a lot of other folks, either. The only people she appeared to like were her family and the few other white people in the community. She was reputed to own hundreds, maybe even thousands, of acres of land, most all of it farmland. She made a fortune, partly because she was able to get cheap labor. Her soil was tilled by black men and women who lived in shacks and to whom she paid a near starvation wage. Not only that, she had a store there that sold snuff and fatback and other cheap goods to those workers so that she got back virtually every penny she paid them.

This lady was beyond thrifty. She was, to use a good southern term, "tight." When she received a letter, she would save the envelope and take it to her store so that when little black boys and girls came in with pennies to buy cookies, she wouldn't "waste" a paper sack. She would place their cookies in her used envelope and send them out the door. Maybe she was difficult because she was afraid. Afraid of her African-American neighbors. Afraid she might lose everything if she were generous.

Those are a couple of my difficult people. You have your own list from your past. We all have, in our present, difficult people with whom we deal. Sometimes those persons are within our own family. It could be a mother-in-law. More often it is a spouse or a child. Or it could be somebody at work or school. It could be a neighbor. It could even be somebody at church.

I remember years ago passing on the outskirts of a town a little sign which read, "Welcome to Troy, Alabama, home of 12,000 warm and wonderful citizens and 2 or 3 old grouches." I could say that about my church! "Welcome to Gulf Breeze United Methodist Church, home of over 3,000 warm and wonderful people and 2 or 3 grouches." I hope the members and guests never let one of those two or three folks get in the way of their relationship with God! Nevertheless, at whatever age or place we are, there are difficult people. Today is the day to consider carefully how to best deal with them.

Jesus gave us very good advice in the Sermon on the Mount (Matthew 5:38-41). A lot of people have trouble with this scripture It's one of the most problematic passages in all the Bible. We have a difficult time with it because it talks about turning the other cheek and going the second mile and loving your enemies. First of all, we find these instructions difficult to follow but, in addition, we've been told that such actions are not psychologically good for us. Then, too, some folks get hung up on the specifics of the passage: "Does this mean you're never supposed to sue anybody?"

It is better to look beyond the illustrations to the point Jesus is making: don't retaliate; don't seek revenge. His advice is good for two very important reasons. The first is to avoid escalating the conflict, and the second is to avoid unnecessary hurt.

When I was growing up, a favorite radio program was "Amos and Andy." I thought it was wonderful. It was always funny and very often it contained insights about life. One of the characters was Kingfish, a pompous and outgoing sort of person. Jim Moore recalls a specific episode in which Kingfish greeted Andy, "Hi-ya Andy," and then slapped Andy on the chest.

Andy resented it. He didn't say anything but he just let his anger seethe and build inside. Finally one day he said to Amos, his friend, "I'm gonna get back at the Kingfish."

"Well, how are you gonna do that?" Amos asked.

Andy answered, "I've hidden two sticks of dynamite inside my vest, and this time when Kingfish slaps me on the chest he's gonna blow his hand clean off!"

Andy didn't realize that he would blow his own heart clean out. When you seek revenge, you damage your own heart, spiritually, emotionally—sometimes physically, too.

If we can't seek revenge or retaliate, what then do we do? First, we can examine ourselves. That's not what we are inclined to do. Usually we think it's the difficult person's problem, not ours. But we must face up to the possibility that the barrier to a solution may lie at our door. We may have erected the fence without realizing it.

A wise person once said, "We are never more discontented with others than when we are discontented with ourselves." I've discovered that to be true about me. When I'm unhappy, I find fault with other people. When I'm contented with myself, then I generally am accepting of other people. If *I'm* grouchy and irritable, I know I have a reason and it's a good reason, so I excuse myself. But if *you* are grouchy and irritable, it's because you are not a nice person. We excuse ourselves because of our intention and we convict others because of their behavior. That's not fair, is it?

Wouldn't it be wonderful to be courageous enough to look at ourselves first and find whatever fault may be within before looking to find fault with others? Isn't that what Jesus said? He said, "If you see a speck in someone else's eye, the first thing you do is you look inside your own eye. You'll find a log there, and only after you have removed the log from your own eye can you see clearly enough to remove the speck from the other person's eye." Today let us begin to deal honestly with ourselves, with our own inadequacies, with the barriers that we build, with our own difficulties. Only then are we ready to deal with the other person.

The Bible has two words of wonderfully practical advice here. Two words. The first word is *understand*. Seek to understand the person or, in the words of an old song, "Walk a mile in my shoes. Friend, before you accuse, criticize and abuse, walk a mile in my shoes."

The words of Stephen Covey, the leading business consultant in the country today, are directly out of this understanding of the scriptures. "Seek first to understand, then to be understood." But we do it exactly the opposite, don't we? We seek first to be understood. If we don't get understood, then we keep on seeking to be understood, and we never seek to understand.

Covey offers a graphic picture of the barrier between two people. The person on one side says the reality is convex. The person on the other side says no, the reality is concave. Who is right? They both are. How, then, can their problem ever be solved? It can't, until one of those persons is willing to walk around to where the other stands and see it from that perspective.

Not only the perception but the reality is different from different points of view. It's certainly easier to attack than to understand, and immediately it's more satisfying to get it off your chest. But it's finally more damaging. It is very hard to resent the person you understand. The first thing to do in looking at the person who's difficult is try to understand the context of that person's life. Ask about the factors that might cause this other person to be this way. It could be the stress, the guilt, the feelings of inferiority. It could be anger or health or other problems.

The second word of advice the Bible offers is *accept*. Accept the person you have the difference with. Jesus said it this way: "Love your enemies." We have a hard time with that admonition because we don't understand what he meant. Jesus wasn't saying to be romantically inclined toward that person or to make that person your best friend. He wasn't saying go play golf or tennis with that person. He was saying *accept* that person. Understand what's going on in that person's life, and come to a place of acceptance.

Eric Fromm said what we do is "swap out" love. If you love me, I'll love you back; if you don't love me, I'm not going to love you. If we are Christians, we must find the better way, to arrive at the place where we accept the other person—not necessarily the person's behavior but that person as a human being and as a child of God. When we can do that, some kind of healing very often will occur. I can't promise you that if we do these things the difficult people will become easy, but I can promise you that if you do these things you will become a better person, a more Christlike person.

Michael Wisser is a Jewish cantor at a synagogue in Lincoln, Nebraska. After moving there several years ago he began receiving harassing telephone calls from a neo-Nazi who was the grand dragon of the Ku Klux Klan. Larry Trapp was a man filled with hate. Wisser attempted to understand Trapp so that he might accept him, and he learned that Trapp was a paraplegic because of diabetes. He had lost both of his legs and his father had ridiculed him because of that disability. Now understanding why Trapp was filled with such rage, Michael Wisser was able to respond calmly, so when Trapp would call and spew his venom, Wisser would say, "You know, Larry, one day you are going to have to answer to God for all that hatred."

The day came that Larry Trapp called to say, "Michael, I want to talk to you about the real things of life. Your people have been the subject of prejudice for two thousand years and have been able to endure. How are you able to do it?" They gradually began to get to know each other and to understand each other.

Michael Wisser's family began to help Larry Trapp. Michael's wife, Julie, ran errands and bought groceries for him. Over the course of time, Larry Trapp gave up his hood and his guns. He gave up membership in the Klan and his post as grand dragon. One day he sent a bouquet of flowers to Julie Wisser with a note which read, "Thank you for changing me from a dragon to a butterfly. It takes eyes blessed by God to see the butterfly inside the dragon."

At Larry Trapp's funeral, the eulogy was given by Donna Pope, a black woman whom Larry had previously harassed with telephone calls. She said, "Only God gives the power to sift through the ashes of a very mean world and find a spark of the truly human."

Today is the day for you to begin to deal positively with the difficult people in your life. To put away your desires for retaliation and revenge. To examine your own motivation. To seek to understand the person who is being difficult. And to come to accept that person. Ask God today to give you the power to sift through the ashes of a world that can sometimes be very mean.

Ask God today to help you look beyond the dragon and find the butterfly.

Receiving and Sharing Love
I John 4:7-10

To Clarice: *I love you more than the first day of deer season.*

ða ða ða

To Linda: *I don't need a lottery, too, I've been a millionaire since I met you.*

ða ða ða

To Sarah: *Roses are red, violets are blue, we are lucky to have a grandma like you.*

ða ða ða

To Dad: *Adopting me has made you the best valentine ever. I love you so much.*

ða ða ða

To My Gene: *In this special retirement time of our lives I love you more than I did 37 years ago. You remain my steadfast husband, my lover and friend.*

These personal ads appeared in a local newspaper on February 14. Every year the newspaper encourages people to compose their own Valentines. Some of them are quite creative. This is my favorite one of all:

> **To Theodore**: *You asked me 30 years ago*
> *to be your blushing bride,*
> *You promised furs and diamond rings*
> *and a limo in which to ride.*
> *I made the payments on the ring,*
> *the fur is on the cat.*
> *The bank has repossessed the car,*
> *but I love you still, you rat!*

The same newspaper ran an article describing the romance between Angeline Kirkland and David Fuqua. They were engaged to be married sixty-two years ago, but David got cold feet and backed out of the engagement. Now they find themselves living in the same retirement home in Brewton, Alabama. David, age 89, is again pursuing Angeline, age 78, with vigor. He says "I thought I had Angeline's heart pretty well won, but if it ain't, I'll go to work at it. I have dearly loved that heart but I jumped the track and let it get away from me."

Evidently love has nothing to do with age! Neither has it to do with size or color or income or appearance.

Receiving and Sharing Love

Love is something that matters to us all. It is the strongest force on earth. The Bible itself says there are three qualities that last forever. There is faith and there is hope and there is love, but even of these three, the strongest is love.

The writer of the First Epistle of John goes further than that. In fact, he makes a statement so bold I would venture to say it's the most extraordinary statement in the Bible. Nowhere else does the Bible define God. But First John 4:8 says *God is love*.

God is love.

The incarnation came as a result of that love, God present with us in Jesus. Because we are Christian, we look to Jesus to know how to live our lives. And so in the area of love, as in the rest of life, I suggest that we look at Jesus as our model of how we are to love other people.

Jesus understood that love begins in the heart of God. Love is a river which flows out of God's heart and into the hearts of his ultimate creations—men and women and boys and girls. God demonstrated this love in the beginning and he continues to demonstrate it. When God made human beings, in his great generosity he gave to them freedom and power. But in time you and I and others like us, though we take advantage of those gifts, abused the gifts of power and freedom. Yet God continues to love us.

This kind of love I call "gift" love. It is the kind of love God meant his people to have, not only from him, but from each other. Gift love means I feel love and I want to share it with you. Gift love is from fullness to emptiness. I don't expect anything in return, it doesn't matter if I get anything in return, I simply give it.

Opposite to God's model of love is "need" love. Need love means I'm going to give love to you, but I do so because I need love myself and I'm hoping that I'll get it back from you. Need love is from emptiness to fullness. You probably know of people who seem to be "clutching" and who are possessive. They are afraid that they will never have love or that they will lose it. Their attitude is "I want it, so I will attempt to offer it." The real agenda of those with need love is selfishness.

While *perfect love casts out fear* (First John 4:18), need love is afraid. It's afraid of losing, afraid of not having. But perfect love, which is gift love, casts out fear.

Jesus' love was not "need" love. It was "gift" love. Jesus loved people from fullness to emptiness. A good example is the woman at the well in Samaria. He said, "I'm going to give you water which will keep you from ever being thirsty again. You will never have to be needy for love again. Because flowing out of the heart of God there is this channel, this river of love which flows through me and into you and it will meet your need."

It's said that love is blind, but only toxic love is blind. Real love is realistic. Real love is without illusion. Real love sees what is actually there.

The theologian Martin Marty tells about an eight-year-old who was asked what a "grandmother" is. Back came this defining statement: "Grandmothers are usually fat, but not too fat to tie up your shoelaces. They wear glasses and sometimes they take out their teeth. They can answer any question, like 'Why do dogs hate cats?' and 'Why isn't God married?' Everybody should try to have a grandmother, especially those who don't have television." That little boy had a realistic kind of love. He didn't see illusion, he saw fact.

During the anguished events leading to Jesus' crucifixion, Simon Peter came to him and said, "Lord, you can count on me. I'm here, I'll always be here for you. I'm with you. When everybody else leaves, I'll be here."

Then Jesus smiled, put his hand on Peter's shoulder and said, "No you won't. You'll be the first one to leave." But he loved Simon Peter anyway. Jesus didn't love people because they measured up, nor did he deceive himself into thinking that their real weaknesses did not exist. He loved them without illusion. He saw beyond the appearance to the reality and he loved them still. The love which Jesus had and which he commends to us begins in the heart of God and flows then to us. It's gift love, not need love. It's from fullness to emptiness. This love is limitless. This kind of limitless love eventually cost Jesus his life.

In Austin, Texas, a Baptist minister received a call from a young man who said that he and his wife had just had a baby. "Preacher, could you come to the hospital to be with us when my wife first sees our baby? He is perfect in every way except that he has no ears. The auditory openings and all the inner-ear parts are there, so he will hear perfectly, but the outer fleshy part is missing. The doctor has told me that when our baby is fully grown and if a donor can be found, an operation could be performed to give him a normal appearance."

The minister went to the hospital with the young man, and they did the best they could to help the mother through the situation.

You can imagine that growing up was tough on that little kid. Sometimes cruel children made fun of him. Many afternoons he came home from school to take refuge in his mother's arms crying, "I'm a freak." But that little boy was so loved, so nurtured and cared for by his parents that he became an excellent student, graduated as valedictorian of his high school class, and went off to college to study geology. One day there was an urgent call at his dormitory from his father, who told him that a donor had been found. The surgery was performed successfully, and it did wonders for this young man's self-esteem. For the first time in his life he felt whole. He was happier than he had ever been.

After graduating from college with honors, he went on to graduate school in a distant city. Another urgent telephone call from his father broke the news that his mother had suffered a severe heart attack. Two nights later at the funeral home, this father and this son stood beside the casket of their wife and mother.

"There is something I must show you," the father said. And he bent over the casket and gently pushed back

Today is the Only Day!

her hair so that the boy could see that his mother had no outer ears. The father said softly, "She made me promise not to tell you."

Like this young man, you and I are the beneficiaries of sacrificial love. This sacrificial love can make all the difference in your life and mine. But it makes all the difference only if we are willing to receive it and only if we are willing to give it. This sacrificial love which flows like a river out of God's heart and into your heart—will you receive it today? This love that can fill you up, will you pass it on today so that that river of love flows from you to others, as well? Will you do that for your sake, and for the sake of a world that needs it so desperately?

Today is the only day you have.

Getting Through to Loved Ones

Ephesians 4:25-32

One of the most important things ministers do is premarital counseling. During my hours with couples we talk about communication, how feelings and needs can be communicated each to the other. Following the wedding ceremony I often receive thank you notes from these young couples, expressing their gratitude. One minister reports receiving a note that said: "We want to thank you for the beautiful way you brought our happiness to a conclusion."

The Bible has many insights about communicating with those we love. Chapters four through six of Ephesians comprise a communications seminar. Chapter four deals principally with general guidelines for communicating our feelings to our loved ones. The next two chapters deal more specifically with husbands and wives, parents and children, employers and employees. If you take these teachings seriously, then you can do a better job of communicating your real feelings and needs to those who are near to you.

This scripture has excellent guidelines. Don't *assign* responsibility; *take* responsibility for what you can do to repair or improve relationships with your significant people. These verses tell you and me what *we* are to do in our relationships, not what we should expect others to do. The assumption is that if you do what you are supposed to in relating to the people near to you, then those relationships will improve.

Most of us operate from the opposite premise. We want to tell the other person what he or she needs to do to change so that the relationship can be better. But we simply do not have that ability.

I operated for years as a parent with the assumption that if my children would cut their hair the way I wanted them to, our relationship would improve. And, to tell the truth, it would have! As I long as I had absolute power I could achieve whatever results I wanted in the context of the relationship. But when children reached a certain age and power became more equal, I couldn't produce that result anymore. I couldn't control their responses and yet I was still trying to make the relationship dependent upon *what they did* rather than upon *what I did*.

One day, as I was leaning over my desk, a button dropped off my shirt. I'm sure that button had been loose for a month. I'd been aware that it was loose. I'd probably worn that shirt three or four times during that month. Every time I put it on, I thought, this button is not tight enough. Every time I put it on, I was aware that it was looser than the last time I wore it.

Why did I wait and let the button fall off? I don't know. Did I assume the button fairy was going to come and secure it tightly to my shirt? Did I assume that Barbara would go to the closet and search through all my shirts and make sure every button was fastened securely? Whatever my thinking process was, I didn't do what I could have done to take the initiative to secure it. I didn't take responsibility.

That button is such a small thing, and it doesn't have anything to do with relationships. But it reminds me to ask, "Who has responsibility for making the changes that need to be made in my significant relationships?" The Bible says I do. I have that responsibility and I am to take it. But it seems easier to choose the opposite, to try to make a relationship better by telling the other person how they need to change so that things can improve.

If the other person is going to change for the better—and some of them won't—it will be only because you and I begin to take responsibility for what we can do to improve that relationship. That's the first principle: don't *assign* responsibility, *take* responsibility for what you can do.

It's important to operate the same way in our relationship with God. If we are feeling apart from God, we know God won't change. It's up to us to come and say, Lord, I will change. I ask nothing of you. I simply will be the person you want me to be, no strings attached. I will take the responsibility.

Taking responsibility means getting rid of bad feelings. St. Paul says exactly that: *get rid of bitterness, passion and anger.* It's amazing to me how insignificant differences can escalate into major warfare. Persons are different, and because we're different we sometimes have bad feelings, even for the people we love. But we can't dump those feelings on the other person. If I want to get rid of garbage, I can't just stack it up in the garbage pail. If I continue to do that, then the pile gets higher and higher. It smells worse and worse and it breeds germs.

To get rid of the garbage means it has to be taken out and away. So it is with bad feelings in any relationship. You have to get those bad feelings outside yourself, but you also have to get them outside the relationship.

Paul tells us how. He says to *speak the truth in a spirit of love*. Say your bad feelings in a positive way, taking responsibility for them yourself and not assigning them to the other person. There are two ways to try to solve a relational problem. You can either attack or you can invite. If you attack, one of two things will happen. Fight or flight. Now, I'm a fighter. So if you attack me, you can count on my attacking you back. Some people are runners: you attack them and they are going to flee. Regardless of which response is made, the relationship suffers. You attack, you get attacked back, the fight escalates and the enmity increases. Or you attack, the other person runs and the distance between you increases. If you attack the other person, only two things can happen and both of them are detrimental.

On the other hand, you could crawl out of your own foxhole into the open space between you and risk being shot at, while trusting that the other person will crawl out of his or her foxhole and meet you at the center to resolve the problem. It may not work. You may get wounded because you crawled out there and made yourself vulnerable. But you will have tried the only thing that ever works: initiating and inviting.

The Apostle says get rid of your bad feelings, get them outside yourself, get them outside the relationship, and invite the other person or persons to help you resolve the feeling problem you have. Emphasize the good aspects, the good qualities of the relationship. Paul says this very clearly. *Do not use harmful words, only helpful words, the kind that build up.* He seems to emphasize the word "only" in that passage. Only words that build up. Because good feelings in relationships are like snowballs rolling down a hill and getting larger and larger, they build. If you focus on a problem, what you see is *problem*: my problem with my brother, my problem with my sister, with my child, with my parent, with my spouse. On the other hand, to focus on the good things, as Paul instructs us to do, allows us to view the situation holistically.

I saw recently a fascinating report of a survey done in Bonn, Germany. A group of psychologists, physicians, and insurance company representatives had come together to do a research project to discover the secret of long-life and success. Participants were asked if they kissed their spouses each morning when they went to work. Seriously! These meticulous German researchers discovered that men who kiss their wives every morning have fewer automobile accidents than those who don't. The kissers report less sickness than the non-kissers. The kissers earned twenty to thirty percent more money than the non-kissers. When asked to explain these findings, Dr. Arthur Zabo said, "A husband who kisses his wife every morning begins the day with a positive attitude."

How does Paul account for good results in maintaining relationships? Keep the approach positive and things are bound to improve.

How did God finally get through to us? When God wanted to express his love for us and his unity with us, what message did he ultimately use? He used plagues and floods, threats and thou-shalt-not's—early Old Testament strategy, right? No, when God wanted to say his ultimate word to us about his desire for closeness and unity with us, he gave his very best, the broken body and the shed blood of his very own. If we offer our best today, taking the responsibility for our side, good things will happen in our relationships with our significant people. Today is the only day we have to initiate a loving break-through.

Seeing and Seizing the Future

Numbers 13 (selected verses)

The majority report came first. Ten of the twelve spies said: "It's a beautiful land, it's a wonderful land, it's rich and fertile. However, the people live in fortified cities and, not only that, they are giants and we saw ourselves as like grasshoppers in their sight. Therefore, we shouldn't try to take the land."

The minority report was given by two out of twelve of Moses' spies, Caleb and Joshua. They said, "It's true the land is wonderful and the fruit is rich and the land is fertile. It's also true that the cities are fortified and the people are like giants. However, if God is with us, we will take this land and occupy it. Therefore, we must not be afraid."

That is a section of one of my favorite Bible stories—how Moses and the Israelites, after they had escaped from Egypt and Pharaoh, have made their way to the brink of the Promised Land. Their forces are poised right at the southern tip of Canaan, the land that God has promised them. Moses sends twelve spies into that land to make sure that the land is good and fertile and to discover what the people are like. The spies are gone for forty days. When they return, with all the people gathered around, they offer their two reports.

Now you can imagine which report the people chose. They went with the majority. After all, it was ten to two. A short time later a feeble effort was made to get into the Promised Land, but it would be years and years before the Israelites were able to seize their destiny, the land of Canaan, because they were afraid.

That's the story and the outcome. There are two basic life truths in that passage. The first is: Fear focuses on the strength of the enemy. The majority said, "We saw giants there. We felt as small as grasshoppers." Fear minimizes our strength and maximizes the strength of the enemy.

Here's the second truth: Faith focuses on God's strength. Caleb and Joshua said, "If the Lord is pleased with us, he will take us there and give us that rich and fertile land, so don't be afraid."

Do you hear the difference? Fear focuses on the obstacles; faith focuses on the opportunities. Those are life principles, and they are applicable in your life and mine, in every context. They are true in home life, they are true in work life, and they are true in the church. Fear will focus on the strength of the enemy and minimize one's own strength. But faith will focus on God's strength and the knowledge that His strength and ours together will enable whatever needs to be done.

At the back of many Bibles you can find a map of Egypt and Sinai at the time of the Exodus. At the upper left-hand corner of the map will be the city of Rameses, in the Nile Delta in Egypt. This is where the Hebrews began their journey from slavery to freedom. Follow along the Mediterranean Sea, along the Wilderness of Shur, and on to Jerusalem, which is in the upper right-hand corner, a distance of a little more than two hundred miles. Ask yourself, how long did it take Moses and the Hebrews to go from Egypt to the Promise Land? The Bible says it took forty years. Why did it take forty years to go two hundred miles? I asked Barbara that question while she was fixing supper. She said, "Because even in that day and time men wouldn't stop and ask directions." Wrong, wrong. That is not the right answer.

The Book of Exodus says that Moses began the journey with 600,000 men who had broken out of slavery. Plus women and children. Assuming there were as many women as men, and assuming there was at least one child for every couple, that makes 1,800,000, and since some of the couples surely had more than one child, there could have been at least two million people on this journey. Can you imagine it? And the Bible tells us that there were sheep and cattle and goats. Can you picture that scene? Two million of them, sheep, cattle, goats, men, women and children straggling across the wilderness. Had Moses decided to go alone or with a smaller group, they could have gotten there swiftly. Had he decided to take a commando group of selected forces, he could have covered the distance in no time. But Moses knew he had to take everybody with him to the Promised Land. He even had to take the whiners and the complainers, the doubters. Everybody.

Can you imagine a better picture of every church across the country? God has set before us a vision of where we need to be and what we need to accomplish as His church and we have to take everybody. We don't have two million in the church where I am pastor, but we have over three thousand, and we must all go together to God's future.

In local churches everywhere the people of God must conquer fear and move forward with faith. Those with vision and those without it must go. The leaders and the followers, the encouragers and the complainers. We are very, very much like the children of Israel in this sense.

Some time ago I was with a group of tourists who worshiped in St. Stephen Cathedral in the city of Vienna. It is the great mother church of all Austria and one of the most beautiful and famous in the whole world. As we prepared for worship, I recalled that during World War II, when the Nazis occupied Austria, a great deal of damage was done, particularly in the city of Vienna, by allied bombers. St. Stephen Cathedral was almost destroyed. When the war ended and Austria was free, Vienna had to be rebuilt. The people had to decide whether to begin with important infrastructure like roads and bridges or with factories and businesses to provide jobs and income for families or with homes and apartments for people to find shelter in. The decision was to begin by rebuilding St. Stephen's. The people understood that it was their spiritual center and that unless they started at the spiritual center they could not find their way to God's dream for them.

Such a vision for the future—based on faith and not fear—is necessary for all individuals who are to reach the land of promise.

Joel Parker, in a video entitled "The Power of Vision," tells of an unprecedented speech given to a sixth grade class. In 1981 Eugene Lang spoke at Public School 121 in Harlem. He had graduated from that school in 1933, had become a successful businessman, and was fairly well-known. He had been invited to speak to that class of fifty-two sixth graders at their commencement exercises. As Eugene Lang sat on the platform and prepared to make his speech, he looked out at those kids and began to realize what a devastating effect their environment had had on them. Then and there he changed his speech, and by so doing changed the destiny of those fifty-two kids.

He told the children that he was present when Martin Luther King, Jr., delivered his famous "I Have A Dream" speech and talked about how important it is to have a dream, how necessary it is to be able to visualize the future, to visualize what you want to become and then to build a pathway to that future. He told them how important it is for them to get a college education. When he looked out at the blank stares on those kids' faces, Eugene Lang knew that this was a totally foreign concept to most of them. He knew they wouldn't go to college. In a moment of divine inspiration Lang said, "I will pay for your college education, every cent of it, for as long as you are there." Fifty-two kids. The speech made headlines across the country because a man was promising a college education to fifty-two kids he didn't know.

Lang knew that it wasn't enough just to give them a vision. He had to also give them the pathway to the dream. To begin the process he set up support groups of teachers, family and friends. It's been more than fifteen years since Lang made that spectacular offer, long enough to track the results. A study of similar sixth grade classes indicates that of this particular class only one-fourth of them could be expected to finish high school. None of them could be expected to go to college!

Today is the Only Day!

In actuality, forty-eight of the fifty-two graduated from high school and forty of them went to college. The difference was that those kids were given a clear vision of their future, so they began to focus on opportunity and not on fear.

The sooner persons can move toward the future, the better, of course. To drag one's feet, as the Israelites surely did, can mean missed opportunities. I think of lines from Shakespeare's *Julius Caesar*, which are prophetic.

> There is a tide in the affairs of men,
> Which, taken at the flood, leads on to fortune;
> Omitted, all the voyage of their life
> Is bound in shallows and in miseries.

For a whole generation the Israelites wandered at the edge of their promised land, "bound in shallows and in miseries." The flood tide of opportunity had come and gone without them. How many todays slipped by before they saw and seized their future? It was the fear of the fight ahead that overwhelmed and immobilized the ancient Israelites.

What is the fear that keeps you from moving out of "the shallows"? May you accept the faith God gives you to set sail on that tide which Shakespeare mentions, the one that leads to God's Promise. It is time today to shed fear, embrace God's strength, and reach for the opportunity. Today is the day to seize the future.